CAMBRIDGE LIBRARY COLLECTION

Books of enduring scholarly value

History

The books reissued in this series include accounts of historical events and movements by eye-witnesses and contemporaries, as well as landmark studies that assembled significant source materials or developed new historiographical methods. The series includes work in social, political and military history on a wide range of periods and regions, giving modern scholars ready access to influential publications of the past.

Travels in the Island of Cyprus

The Abbé Giovanni Mariti wrote an account of the condition of Cyprus in 1769, almost 100 years after the final conquest conquest of the island by the Ottoman Turks. Mariti travelled widely around the island in the seven years during which he served there as a consular official, and as well as recounting his own visits to towns, villages and monasteries, he describes contemporary events such as the outbreak of plague in 1760 and the failed insurrection against the Turks in 1764. This English translation, first published in 1895, also provides contemporary eye-witness accounts of the sieges of Nicosia and Famagusta which ended Venetian rule in 1570-1, and of the torture and death of the Venetian commander of Famagusta, Marcantonio Bragadino, a story which has passed into legend.

T0381655

Cambridge University Press has long been a pioneer in the reissuing of out-of-print titles from its own backlist, producing digital reprints of books that are still sought after by scholars and students but could not be reprinted economically using traditional technology. The Cambridge Library Collection extends this activity to a wider range of books which are still of importance to researchers and professionals, either for the source material they contain, or as landmarks in the history of their academic discipline.

Drawing from the world-renowned collections in the Cambridge University Library, and guided by the advice of experts in each subject area, Cambridge University Press is using state-of-the-art scanning machines in its own Printing House to capture the content of each book selected for inclusion. The files are processed to give a consistently clear, crisp image, and the books finished to the high quality standard for which the Press is recognised around the world. The latest print-on-demand technology ensures that the books will remain available indefinitely, and that orders for single or multiple copies can quickly be supplied.

The Cambridge Library Collection will bring back to life books of enduring scholarly value across a wide range of disciplines in the humanities and social sciences and in science and technology.

Travels in the Island of Cyprus

With Contemporary Accounts of the Sieges of
Nicosia and Famagusta

GIOVANNI MARITI

CAMBRIDGE
UNIVERSITY PRESS

CAMBRIDGE UNIVERSITY PRESS

Cambridge New York Melbourne Madrid Cape Town Singapore São Paolo Delhi

Published in the United States of America by Cambridge University Press, New York

www.cambridge.org
Information on this title: www.cambridge.org/9781108004329

© in this compilation Cambridge University Press 2009

This edition first published 1909
This digitally printed version 2009

ISBN 978-1-108-00432-9

TRAVELS

IN THE

ISLAND OF CYPRUS

CAMBRIDGE UNIVERSITY PRESS WAREHOUSE,
C. F. CLAY, Manager.

London: FETTER LANE, E.C.
Edinburgh: 100, PRINCES STREET.

Berlin: A. ASHER AND CO.
Leipzig: F. A. BROCKHAUS.
New York: G. P PUTNAM'S SONS.
Bombay and Calcutta: MACMILLAN AND CO., Ltd.

TRAVELS

IN THE

ISLAND OF CYPRUS

TRANSLATED FROM THE ITALIAN OF

GIOVANNI MARITI

BY

CLAUDE DELAVAL COBHAM, C.M.G.

B.C.L., M.A. UNIV. COLL. OXON.

*WITH CONTEMPORARY ACCOUNTS OF THE SIEGES OF
NICOSIA AND FAMAGUSTA*

Cambridge:
at the University Press
1909

Cambridge:

PRINTED BY JOHN CLAY, M.A.
AT THE UNIVERSITY PRESS.

PREFACE

THE Ottoman Conquest of Cyprus in 1571 found, no less than the British Occupation of 1878, a goodly number of chroniclers, some of them eyewitnesses of the events which they described.

Of the three hundred years which elapsed between these two noteworthy dates in Cypriot history we know very little. Visitors came and went, complained of the heat and the discomforts of travel, and commented with more or less acumen on the information which filtered to them through their interpreters.

But to two writers we can appeal as authorities, both residents, intelligent men, and directly interested in knowing the true condition of the island. The first, the Abbé Giovanni Mariti, was for some years an official of the Imperial and Tuscan Consulates, and published at Lucca in 1769 his *Viaggi per l' isola di Cipro*. The second, Cyprianos, a native, and Archimandrite of the archbishop of Cyprus, published at Venice in 1788 his *Chronological History of the Island of Cyprus*. I have printed in the *Excerpta Cypria* a translation into English of the account given by the latter of Cypriot affairs between 1571 and 1788. In the present volume I have given an exact rendering of the former, adding (in Chapters XXVI—XXVIII) in a rather more compressed form the substance of Chapters IX—XI of the second volume of

Mariti's later work *Viaggio da Gerusalemme per le coste della Soria* (Livorno, 1787).

My task was nearly done when I obtained copies of the anonymous versions in French (Paris, 1791) and English (London, 1791). Both are scarce books, but even were this not so I should not regret the trouble I have taken in placing before the reader an accurate rendering of the Italian original. The French translator scarcely pretends to follow Mariti's text, and tries to cover the bareness of his author's narrative with purple patches of his own, impertinent or superfluous. The Englishman renders literally from the Frenchman, without a hint that he has never seen the Italian original. (See pp. 3, 36, 44, 55, 65, 251, &c.) I have not seen the German version by C. G. Hase, Altenburg, 1777.

The Abbé Mariti arrived in Cyprus from Leghorn February 2, 1760, and left it on his return to Florence, October 6, 1767. His work owes little to previous writers on Cyprus: he had read Bordone, Lusignan and probably Meursius, but he relies almost entirely on his own notes of what he had seen and heard. And herein lies its value, for he is observant and conscientious. The book stands as the best account of the condition of Cyprus in the third quarter of the last century, and as such I leave it, hardly attempting by additions or corrections to bring it up to date. I have left most names of places in his own spelling, indicating in the index, which is new, their present equivalents. Turkish words appear as modern Oriental scholars would have them transcribed.

The Piastre of Mariti's time was equal to 3 *lire*, 6 *soldi*, 8 *danari*, Florentine money, which we may reckon as 3 francs (French) or half a crown (English) of that day. The *oke* (now $2\frac{4}{5}$ Eng. lbs.) was $3\frac{3}{4}$ Florentine pounds: the *cantar* (180 Cyprus okes) was 100 *rotoli* of $6\frac{7}{8}$ Fl. lbs. (or $687\frac{1}{2}$ Florentine pounds): the *couza* (now 9 English quarts) contained 5 Florentine *fiaschi*: 4 *couze* or 20 *fiaschi* making a *barile*.

It would be well that as many as possible of the original

sources of Cypriot history were made accessible to Englishmen in their own tongue. Of so desirable a work I offer this volume as a small instalment. But that dedications are out of date it would certainly be inscribed, with affectionate respect, to F. M. VISCOUNT WOLSELEY, under whose wise and spirited rule Cyprus entered on a new era of peace and prosperity.

LARNACA, *December* 12, 1895.

NOTE TO THE SECOND EDITION

For this second edition I have recast Chap. III with the help of Mariti's later *Dissertation on the Ancient City of Citium* (Livorno, 1787), the rest of which I have condensed as Chapter XXIX.

Mariti's scheme allowed no more than a couple of pages to the Sieges of Nicosia and Famagusta, so I hope the reader will welcome the two narratives with which, by way of an appendix, I have completed the volume. I prefix to them notes on their authors, as well as on other less known accounts of these most noteworthy events.

C. D. C.

THE ATHENÆUM,
October 1, 1908.

CHAPTER I.

A GENERAL VIEW OF THE ISLAND AND KINGDOM OF CYPRUS.

CYPRUS, an island in the Mediterranean Sea, and dependency of Turkey in Asia, lies in long. 52° 45′ and lat. 35° 30′, between the coast of Syria and that of Cilicia now called Caramania. It has had various names. Pliny, v. 31, calls it Acamantis, Cerastis, Aspelia, Amathusia, Macaria, Cryptos and Colinia. In other historians it bears the names of Chetinia, Aerosa, Paphos, Salamina; and in the poets Cythera, from the goddess Venus who, they say playfully, was there nursed and brought up, and to whom were erected there several temples, of which the most conspicuous were in the cities of Paphos, Cythera and Amathus. Cyprus once comprised nine kingdoms—"quondam novem regnorum sedem" says Pliny, afterwards the Kings of Egypt reigned there, and then the Romans. From the Empire of the West it passed to that of the Greek Emperors of Constantinople, from whom it was wrested by the Arabs in the days of Heraclius. The Emperors soon recovered their sovereignty, but Isaac, a prince of the family of the Comneni, who ruled the island with the title of Duke, usurped the supreme power, and through the weakness of the Empire remained in absolute and peaceful possession, until in 1191 Richard I, King of England, took his throne and his life, and sold the kingdom to the Knights Templars. These, owing to their harsh behaviour towards the natives who followed the Greek rite, saw that they could not

I

long hold it in peace, and were obliged to restore it to Richard, who made over his rights to Guy Lusignan. Carlotta, the last scion of that family, was expelled in 1460 by her natural brother Jacques. She married Louis of Savoy, through whom those Dukes take the title of Kings of Cyprus. Jacques died, and his widow Carlotta Cornaro being childless gave the kingdom to the Venetians in 1489. They could not hold it against the Turks, who took it from them in 1570, and still hold it undisturbed. Ferdinand de' Medici, Grand Duke of Tuscany, attempted the conquest of the island, and might have succeeded, say the historians, had he been better served by the commander of his forces.

This most beautiful island has a circuit (including its bays) of 600 miles. It is 200 miles long, and 65 broad, and is crossed and divided by a range of mountains running from east to west: the highest of these are Olympus, S. Croce and Buffavento.

The greatest of her plains is that of Mesaria, of 78 miles in length, and 30 in breadth.

Her streams and torrents which flow even in winter are but few, so subject is the island to drought. It is said that in the days of Constantine the Great no rain was seen for full thirty years, and the land lost many of its inhabitants.

In ancient times there were many cities, but now the names only of a few remain attached to their old sites; of the rest the very locality is forgotten. The notable towns which still exist are Nicosia and Famagusta, which rank as walled cities. One might add Larnaca, where are the European mercantile houses. There are also seven large forts, in each of which is a *Disdar* or Commandant.

Cyprus surpasses every other Greek island in the number of natives illustrious for their birth, dignity, learning and saintliness. Strabo, *Geography*, XIV. 20, says of the island " κατ' ἀρετὴν οὐδεμίας τῶν νήσων λείπεται—it yields to no other island in excellence." Many ancient historians have thought that the air was bad and unwholesome, a prejudice which causes foreigners to stay here a short time so that they cannot fully test its climate. But it is the general opinion of all who have lived here some few years that the air is good. The tertian and quartan fevers which are seen to prevail so frequently and for so long a time not only in Cyprus but also throughout the Levant, spring from causes other and more avoidable than the air. I learnt from experience that I myself gave occasion to the relapses which made this malady hang about me for quite ten months. The great heat causes constant and copious perspirations, and with these upon one to expose oneself to the least draught produces a check, which is followed inevitably the next day by a fever. The use of strong drinks is another cause, and the free use of certain fruits, particularly cucumbers, pumpkins and water-melons, which are difficult to digest. The villagers everywhere suffer often from these fevers, especially in summer; they let blood and leave the cure to nature without a change of diet except that they abstain from fruit. But this treatment is not enough for Europeans, who have to be more careful lest the malady grow more severe. A relapse can be avoided by taking sparingly of any food, and if this is not effective, riding is a remedy of approved excellence: at least it keeps off the obstructions which frequently follow this kind of fever. Turks and Greeks use the same treatment; the latter, wearied sometimes of the tiresome persistence of the disease, after the fourth or fifth attack have recourse to a large potion of the excellent and generous wine of the island, which usually cures most of them, if taken just when the shiverings point to an early recurrence of the fever.

There are various religions current in the land for, although it is ruled by Muslims, Islam is not the prevailing faith, most of the inhabitants being schismatic Greeks. There are many Armenians, then come the Maronites who observe their own rites in the matter of feasts and fasts, but having no churches of their own they officiate, and fulfil the duties of Catholic Christians, in the Latin churches. The number of Latin Catholics is much smaller than that of the sects named above, for they are only the Europeans settled in the island, among whom are the fathers of St Francis (Minori Observanti) called *Padri di Terra Santa*, the name I shall give them in my book, for they are known by it throughout the Levant.

The Turks have a *Molla*, who ranks as the head of their Law; the Greeks an archbishop and three bishops; the Maronites an archpriest, and the Latins two curates, one for the French, another for the Italian colony, everyone being free to follow his own religion.

The English have neither church nor house of prayer, but when they are in sufficient numbers they would assemble in the house of their consul, and then they would be obliged to maintain a minister of their religion; but such is now wanting.

Greek and Turkish are the common languages, with the result that both one and the other are corrupted. Greek has here perhaps adhered with greater purity to the ancient vocabulary, but the pronunciation is entirely spoiled: an effect, they say, of the Venetian domination. The Greek commercial class frequently use Italian, French very little indeed. It is very remarkable that all orientals learn our Italian tongue with more ease than the other languages of Europe.

The Cypriots are generally well formed, tall and good looking, sober and temperate. The women have mostly good eyes, but ugly features, and few are seen of any special beauty : they are tall, spirited, little industrious, and luxurious :- they are long lived, and often re-marry when they are already great-grandmothers. All Greeks like amusement, but the Cypriots to excess; and though they be never so much oppressed by the government they never lose their liveliness.

The men dress *alla Turca*, like those of Constantinople,

and so too the women of any position, except as to the adornment of the head, which is high and striking, a fashion of very ancient date, which they say has been preserved here more faithfully than in the other Greek islands. Their general costume, *alla Cipriotta*, is more scanty than the other *alla Turca*; it consists of a kind of tight vest, and a skirt of red cotton cloth, the outer garment, which they call *benisce* (Turkish, *binish*) is of cloth, velvet or other silk stuff. This is a long mantle, which starts from the shoulders, and passing over the arms, almost reaches the ground. It is not closed in front, but leaves the body exposed down to the feet. The under garments are of silk, made in the country, and like white veils. They have drawers reaching to the feet, and their boots, called *mesti* (Turkish, *mest*), are a kind of low boots of yellow leather, which reach to the instep, under which they wear slippers. They wear no stays, but a little corset of dimity, which stops below the bosom, the rest being covered only by that plain, fine chemise, and another small piece of stuff which they wear for greater modesty. They adorn their necks and arms with pearls, jewels and gold chains. Their head dress, of which I have spoken above, consists of a collection of various handkerchiefs of muslin, prettily shaped, so that they form a kind of casque of a palm's height, with a pendant behind to the end of which they attach another handkerchief folded in a triangle, and allowed to hang on their shoulders. When they go out of doors modesty requires that they should take a corner and pull it in front to cover the chin, mouth and nose. The greater part of the hair remains under the ornaments mentioned above, except on the forehead where it is divided into two locks, which are led along the temples to the ears, and the ends are allowed to hang loose behind over the shoulders. Those who have abundance of hair make as many as eight or ten plaits. Cypriot women like sweet odours about their heads, and to this end adorn them grotesquely with flowers. The Christian ladies when they go abroad make a great parade of their costumes, while the Turks are covered from head to foot with a white cotton sheet.

The realm of Cyprus was governed for many years by a Pasha, sent by the Ottoman Porte, but the island began to decline from its ancient splendour, and the necessary cost of the maintenance of a Pasha and his court being found to weigh heavily on the people, they petitioned that the practice might be abolished, and that henceforth they might have instead a *Muhassil* or simple governor, which was at once granted to them. But they soon found the government of a *Muhassil* to be burdensome, and some years ago begged that they might have a Pasha again. This was refused, and they still find themselves under a yoke which at one time they thought less oppressive.

The revenues of the country are left to the Vezir A'zam, grand Vezir or Lieutenant of the Ottoman Empire. But as he cannot come here to rule it himself, he grants the island to the highest bidder, and sends him to govern it with a *Khatti Sherif* or august writing, a special order of the Grand Signor, bearing his autograph.

As it is not merit but interest which gives access to this dignity, it is by interest that the governors regulate their actions. They ill-use and harass the people, and impose on them unjust taxes, not only to recoup what they pay to the Grand Vezir but also enough to allow them to leave the country after a year, having made their own fortunes and those of all their train. As the Grand Vezir finds every year in Constantinople men who offer more to get the reins of this kingdom, Cyprus is reduced to a miserable condition for want of money, and of a large yield of its usual rich products— results which follow the abandonment of their country by thousands of its inhabitants, one of the greatest disgraces of a state. In all the Turkish dominions there is probably no place where the dues paid by their subjects are heavier;

amounting, as they sometimes do, to 200 piastres, which make 100 Florentine scudi yearly per head, without distinction of larger or smaller means. The mere *Kharaj* or poll tax, imposed by the Grand Signor on his subjects, is only five piastres, while here it was increased to 40 piastres a head. And the people had to consider it a special favour that after many representations and petitions they were able to obtain a favourable rescript that they should not be bound or compelled to pay more than 21 piastres a head. In the year 1764 the tyranny of Chil Osman Agha, the Governor, had reached its height, and the people, the lower class of Turks especially, having grown insolent, committed the detestable excess of killing him, a deed which was soon followed by lamentable consequences, as I shall show in the proper place. I shall give a particular account of these events, at which I was present, and I had besides occasion to be mixed up with the leaders in the negotiations which were conducted by the Tuscan consul.

The suite of the *Muhassil* is composed of the *Khasnadar* or treasurer, the *Kiaya* or secretary, and other subaltern charges entrusted to the *Chawushes* who are his personal guards, and the *Choqadars*, men about the court, who have different duties. Their number is not fixed, but there are generally from 100 to 150, and they have their own chiefs called *Bash-Chawush* and *Bash-Choqadar*. There are besides the *Sarafs*, through whose hands pass all the monies which enter or leave the Treasury, their duty being to test its goodness and value, and to keep the accounts. This office is held by a Greek, and the *Terjuman* of the *Serai*, or interpreter of the Palace, is also a Greek, who holds his post by a firman or order of the Porte.

When the Governor wishes to impose some tax on the Greek *ri'aya*, or subjects, he does not address himself to the people directly, but to the interpreter, and he to the archbishop, who sends notice to the several dioceses to make the most convenient arrangements to avoid annoyances or to lessen the demand. The poor subjects might very often be saved from oppression if their archbishop were not from policy, and sometimes from personal interest, ready to lend himself to the exactions of the *Muhassil*, so that they are often abandoned by the very person who ought to take their part. When the Governor wishes to collect money out of season, or of his mere caprice, the mode of imposing duties and taxes is curious enough. He may even tax with a certain sum anyone who bears a name which he may select; as, for instance, anyone called George has, without appeal, to pay a certain sum. Such an exaction falls on members of the Greek community only, who are treated more as slaves than subjects.

For voluntary homicide the law imposes on the slayer the capital penalty, and on the village where the homicide took place a tax which goes to the treasury of the Grand Signor, together with the sum levied as blood-money. The blood-money for a man killed, of 30 or 35 years of age, is reckoned at 500 piastres: for others a calculation is made of the time which, humanly speaking, the man might have lived, and of the gain which in that residue of his life might have accrued therefrom to the Grand Signor, the sum being often excessive. If the homicide resulted from some accident, or were indirectly planned, the slayer very often escapes all punishment but the payment of some few piastres. The *Mehkeme* are the courts before which are pleaded all causes, criminal and civil; in the capital the *Molla* presides, in the other cities and in the principal villages the *Qazi*, judges who acquit or condemn after a short hearing. The Turks have no written civil law, their guide is the Qur'an, their sacred book. Every good *Qazi* ought to have many texts from it, called *Fetawa*, written out in long lists, to which, according to the cases, are given various interpretations, very often opposed to the true sentiments of their lawgiver.

A man who is summoned to a court for debt has no choice

but to pay to the *Qazi* the tenth part of the sum in dispute:
this is disbursed by the debtor if he is proved to be such, or
by the plaintiff, if his claim be fraudulent or unfounded.
A similar fee of one-tenth falls to the *Qazi* from the property
of every person deceased. But the valuation is not very
strict.

There are in the island of Cyprus 16 *Qaziliqs*, which are
so many courts, in each of which a *Qazi* presides, but all
are subordinate to their chief the *Molla*. For although they
may hold their posts under a special *firman*, or order of the
Porte, they cannot give judgment except in a provisional form.
In affairs of any consequence they must draw up their *i'lam*,
or judgment, and send it to the Governor, who sends it to the
Molla, without whose consent and approval the Governor
cannot examine a matter affecting the life of a subject.

The military government of the island rests with the *Alay
Bey*, who is the General of the *Sipahi* or mounted troops,
and the *Yenicheri Agha*, who commands the infantry: their
captain is called *Zabit* and *Qolaghasi*. There ought to be
3000 *Sipahi* in the island, and about 8000 *Yenicheri* (Janissaries), but now one would hardly find 100 of the first, and
2000 of the last, the several commandants having appropriated
the pay and perquisites of the many men wanting.

When the Turks took the island there were reckoned
80,000 subjects chargeable with the *Kharaj* or poll-tax, not
counting women, children and old men, who were exempt.
This number was maintained as long as the kingdom continued to be prosperous, and the Grand Signor received as his
just due, at five piastres a head, 400,000 piastres a year.

Wealth soon decreased and with it the population, but the
Pashas continued to exact the same sum, and to this end
increased the taxes on those who remained; and this course
was followed even when the government was transferred to a
Muhassil, for these officers raised the amount to 40 piastres
a head. Now there are only 12,000 men liable to *Kharaj*

and this, as I have said above, is reduced to 21 piastres a head, yet the result is the by no means contemptible sum of 252,000 piastres. Add to this as much again extorted by the Governor, the Chief Justices, the officers of every grade, and you have a revenue of 504,000 piastres. So that we may conclude that the population has notably decreased, and the sums wrung from it increased.

The population thus reduced will scarcely amount now to 40,000 souls in all. But the number is extremely hard to fix accurately, not only in Cyprus but in every other province of the Levant, for Eastern peoples keep no registers of births or deaths, and count the inhabitants only by those who pay the poll-tax, who are less than a third of the whole. I ought to add that in Asia the number of women largely exceeds that of men, a fact which I have observed and proved in all the various tribes among whom I have lived in the Levant.

The products of the island were many and rich. In old days there were mines of gold, silver, copper, iron, marcasite (iron pyrites), vitriol and rock-alum: even emeralds have been found here. Of some of these there remains but a memory, and the name of the district where they were found. The existing Turkish government allows no search, and no enterprise for their recovery. It used to make a large quantity of oil and sugar. But cultivation of the sugar-cane had begun to fall off even in the Venetian epoch, as it was found more profitable to plant cotton. Saffron and rhubarb gave no inconsiderable return, but these plants have disappeared. Wild goats, deer, wild boars, wild asses and wild cattle have all been exterminated; as well as pheasants, which abounded in Cyprus even after its unhappy absorption in the Ottoman Empire.

The present products are silk, cotton, wool, madder (called *boia, rizari* and *robbia*), muscat and precious wines, cochineal, ladanum, wheat and barley, colocynth, pitch and tar, potash, salt, carobs, timber, and umber, brown and green; with these articles European commerce, of which I shall speak more fully in its proper place, is chiefly concerned.

The island used to furnish oil in such abundance that it was largely exported: now the produce is so greatly reduced that oil is frequently imported. In no less quantity was found *giuggiolena*, called here *sesame*, from the seeds of which was extracted oil, and as the people of Anatolia still grow it for export to the neighbouring coast of Syria, it used to be a great resource in years when there was a scarcity of olive oil.

The plant *sesame* in height, in its leaves and flowers, is much like that which we call *belluomo*, and from the small seed which remains in the husk after it has reached maturity, is expressed the oil. When the island was thickly peopled, the inhabitants were wont to extract oil from *sondro* (glass wort) also, an expedient they were glad to use when neither olive nor sesame oil sufficed for their wants. In their extreme need they used also the fruit of another plant called *Curtunià* (Palma Christi) which begins to show its fruit while it is quite small, and grows until a man can stand comfortably beneath it: its leaves are starshaped, and the stem reaches a circumference of a foot, but it is always green and soft and sappy. The fruit is as big as a French bean, and is composed, like a chestnut, of husk and skin, and, within, a nut rich in oily matter which is used generally, except as a condiment with food.

The soil produces every kind of edible herb, and other wild plants, the better knowledge of which would be of no small honour to botany. Fruit is rare nowadays, because the trees have been neglected, but the island is rich in flowers, and a very little care suffices to rear and develop the most beautiful and delicate plants of Italy, France and Holland. Without culture there spring of themselves hyacinths, anemones, ranunculi, and double and single daffodils, which have as many as 14 bells on one stalk. They grow on the hills, whence the bulbs are transplanted to adorn our gardens: they are in

great demand in France and Holland, where they are carefully cultivated; many thousands are sent there every year.
The gardens are very rich in all the species of *Citrus*, especially
oranges of an exquisite and most delicate flavour. Among the
wild plants is found the little bee orchis, which we call *fiore
ape*, and the Greeks μέλισσα, from its likeness to a bee. It
sends up one or, at the most, two stalks, and on each stalk
there are five or six flowers: the root is bulbous, and its juice
is used in the cure of wounds.

The Cypriots cultivate a plant which they call *henna*; it
grows to the height and thickness of a pomegranate tree, which
it nearly resembles in its stem and branches, the leaves are
like those of the myrtle; and the flowers like a thick cluster of
the flower of the vine. An oil is extracted from it, whose
virtues are those of balsam. The odour is very pleasing to
orientals, but Europeans find it rank and unbearable. When
the flower has fallen, a fruit is formed like a large coriander
seed. The leaves, dry or fresh, when boiled in water produce
a fine orange dye, with which the Turkish women and a few
Greeks stain their nails and the palms of their hands, with the
idea that it refreshes the body. They dye their hair with it, as
an adornment. And so tenacious is the dye, that it is not
easy except by a long lapse of time to efface it.

The Venetians when they were lords here used to dye their
horses' coats with this colour; now, so far as regards animals,
this custom is confined to white greyhounds and horned cattle.
Since the number of the inhabitants has diminished, a large
part of the island is uncultivated, and yields only thyme and
marjoram. These give a pleasant smell as one passes over
the plains, and are used as brushwood to heat ovens and
furnaces.

In the caves of a mountain near Paphos is found a very
perfect kind of rock crystal, commonly called from its lustre
Paphos diamonds: it is cut and polished like other precious
stones. It is forbidden under severe penalties to carry off the

most minute particle, and to this end guards are set over the spot: but a present will buy some little licence.

The same jealousy is shown about the amiantus, a stone found near the village of Paleandros. Various historians testify that by certain processes cloth was made from it, and that to clean this it was thrown upon the fire, whence it was withdrawn clean and unburnt. Pliny speaks of it, XXXVI. 19, "amiantus, like alum, loses nothing of its substance from fire"; and Dioscorides, v. 158, says of the Cyprian amiantus "there is produced in Cyprus a stone called amiantus, resembling alum (*alumen scissile*), which is prepared and made into a cloth which looks like leather. When thrown into the fire, it burns but comes forth brighter, and is not consumed."

The modern Greeks called the amiantus *carystia*: others, *Cotton-stone*.

Besides this stone there is found also much red jasper, agate and three different kinds of precious stones. The hills nearest to Larnaca are all of talc, from which is prepared the gypsum so generally used in the island.

Of wild quadrupeds there are only foxes and hares: the latter, owing to the fine pasture, are better flavoured than our own. The European residents keep horses and dogs, and amuse themselves greatly at all seasons of the year in hunting these animals.

Among birds the commonest are francolins, partridges, woodcock, quails, thrushes, and every kind of waterfowl: we may say in fact that no winged game is lacking. The price of francolins and of partridges is the same, five soldi each. Woodcocks are a little dearer, for though they are abundant enough they are more prized, and other birds are extremely cheap. I must not forget the beccafico and the ortolan, which are very plump: they are sold indiscriminately at four soldi the bunch of twelve, and they are so plentiful that even at this price they are a source of profit to the villagers. The largest catches are made near Santa Napa. Some are sold fresh, but most of them have the head and feet cut off, are scalded, and then put into vinegar with certain drugs. Thus prepared they keep for a year, and are sold at the same price as the fresh birds. The sale of these little birds is in the hands of the Europeans at Larnaca, who continually receive commissions from England, Holland, France, and some parts of the Turkish dominions, from correspondents who desire them for their own use. Every year 400 little barrels are exported, some containing 200, others 400 birds. The way they are generally prepared here for the table is to cut them in two, and put them on the gridiron with bread crumbs and a little parsley which gives them an excellent flavour.

In the months of July and August one sees many vultures standing in the fields like flocks of sheep; but they are only birds of passage, whilst all the other creatures we have mentioned are natives: unless we should except the woodcock, whose nest has never been found in any part of the island, nor indeed, so they say, elsewhere.

Among the venomous beasts there is a kind of snake, which the Greeks call κουφή, or deaf, whose bite is mortal. The longest are two feet in length, and their thickness across about a thumb's length. They are yellow and black, and have two little horns on the head. The Greeks err in calling it the deaf snake, as it is certainly not deaf, for the peasants when they reap the corn, among which it chiefly lives, to guard themselves from its attacks, besides keeping their boots always on their feet, have also little bells bound to their sickles to alarm and scare them away. A useless precaution, were the snakes really deaf. I ought to add before leaving the subject that at Tremitiu, a village in the island, is a Greek family which is said to enjoy the hereditary virtue of curing persons bitten by these serpents. I have seen myself two persons who within twenty-four hours after the bite presented themselves to one of this family, and by a simple pressure of the wound were healed. On the other hand others have died who did not seek, or who despised, this remedy. But it is true that their virtue consists in a particular secret, for when they press the affected part, they deftly apply some powder which causes severe but momentary pain.

The Tarantula of Cyprus is a spider of dark hue inclining to black, all covered with long hairs. Its bite is very dangerous, but not mortal; it never fails to cause pains accompanied by fever. That of the Galera is poisonous and mortal. This is a narrow beast, flat, about six inches long, of a yellowish hue, and furnished with a quantity of legs which it moves all together like the oars of a galley, whence it takes its name. There is also a black snake five or six feet long. This is not venomous, and may be handled without offence. It is sometimes skinned and cooked, and said to be a savoury morsel.

The horses are not fleet, but in Pafo there is a breed which is renowned for the pace called *chapqun*, a short amble, which they can keep up for six hours running, over hills or plains, without the least inconvenience to the rider. The donkeys have the same pace, and the mules of both sexes, which are considered the finest in this part of the Levant.

The oxen are small and lean; the Greeks do not eat beef, upon the principle that the beast that tills the ground should not be used as food for man.

The sheep supply the best meat. There are some magnificent ones, with a tail so large that it weighs as much as fifty pounds, and some have three and even five horns. The lambs are chiefly eaten in the summer. The flocks of goats are really beautiful on account of the remarkable cleanness of the animals, the different colours and varied spots of their coats.

The greyhounds are much valued for the chase, and their speed is such that when one goes to hunt with falcons, dogs of a slower race are taken, so as not to lose one's pleasure if the hare were caught in the twinkling of an eye. The best breed is white, with long hair about the ears and tail, and a long but stout and strong foot, the rest of the coat being somewhat rough.

The time is past when arts and sciences flourished among the Greeks. Ignorance has taken their place, ignorance reigns. The Mohammadans one and all acknowledge no idol but wealth, and this they seek not by those fair means which the cultivation of the liberal and mechanical arts suggest, but only by violence and tyranny. The kingdom of Cyprus and all Syria—we may except a few parts of Asia and European Turkey—are the touchstone of this truth. In the island of which I speak there are no arts but those which are indispensable to human existence. Or if there are others they are only those concerned with the manufacture of cotton. And these deal with so small a produce that it can no longer keep up a regular commerce with Europe. The same may be said of the manufacture of skins tanned with sumach, yellow, red and black, of which just enough are prepared for home consumption.

Although the Greeks are sunk in idleness and indolence, so far as regards the arts and sciences, they still show signs of talent, and of pride of spirit, which makes one remember what their ancestors were: but few know how to employ these qualities to any good end. They are accomplished only in fraud, deceit and such subtleties that one needs the eyes of Argus to guard oneself from their treachery. Few have any education, and these few are the priests, who learn to read the written language, though but few of them know its real meaning.

Now that I have spoken of and described the island and kingdom of Cyprus in general, I will pass on to particulars.

CHAPTER II.

CONCERNING THE PORT AND TOWN
OF THE SALINES.

THE port of the Salines in the south of the island is the general anchorage for vessels of every nation, not only because it is the best to be found in all the kingdom of Cyprus, but also because it is the nearest to Larnaca, the city which has the greatest trade in all the island.

On the shore is a town called also town of the Salines, whose length is greater than its breadth. It contains a fort built by the Turks in 1625, armed with several good pieces of artillery which bear the arms of the republic of Venice. It is a wretched building, and almost in ruins on the sea side; it has however a guard of Janissaries, and its *Disdar* or Commandant. It is square without any bastion. Now its principal use seems to be to fire salutes to the war vessels of the Christian Powers, and to return those of the Grand Signor's.

A little way from the fort is a Khan, or barrack, which is like a convent for monks, with its various rooms where are received all foreigners who have not their own places of abode, and here they can stay as long as they will at a small expense. Near it is the bazar or market, where are sold eatables, clothes, cloth and so on for men's use. It is the best market of the whole island, and business and sales are the greatest, because all the ships from Syria come here for their provisions, prices, especially of eatables, being moderate. In the shops too are found all kinds of European goods.

Near the bazar is the custom-house, over which is a

Turkish *agha* or gentleman, who is looked upon here as the Customs officer, but really he is a mere deputy of the Chief Collector of the island, who lives in Nicosia.

The merchants are chiefly in this town, where they keep their goods, particularly cotton and wool.

The Greek Christians have here, on the land side of the town, an ancient church of three aisles, dedicated to St Lazarus, who was, they say, bishop of Cyprus, and in a chapel on the right as you enter, going down a short stair, you are shown a sepulchre hollowed out of the rock in which they believe the body of the saint lay. The Greeks throng to it very devoutly, and insist that the body was carried off to Venice. The church originally belonged to the Latin clergy. It was taken from them under an order of the Grand Signor, but they always preserve a right to the side chapel on the left, and twice a year in token of their right the Fathers of Terra Santa go to celebrate the Holy Mysteries there. Within the church there is nothing remarkable, except the pulpit of marble, supported on the emblems of the four evangelists well carved, as well at least as suits the Gothic style in which the rest of the church is built. The font too is worth a look, though it is simple and without ornament. It had four shields of arms which have been hacked away by the Greeks, in their hatred for every little memorial of the Latins which may be found in churches of their rite.

The Greeks baptise by immersion, but use in Cyprus many ceremonies not prescribed in their rituals. They rarely confer this sacrament before the eighth day after birth. A Latin who wished to join their communion must be rebaptised, just as they would rebaptise a Greek who had become a Catholic, and then wished again to return to their church.

The screen which divides the choir from the *Sancta Sanctorum*, in this church of St Lazarus, as in all churches of the Greek rite, is made of wood carved and gilded, and adorned with various pictures of saints, painted on wood, as the Greeks must not adore any figure in relief which represents our Lord, or the Virgin Mary or the saints.

In every Greek church is an episcopal throne, which stands at the entrance of the choir, but always on the left side (*in cornu epistolae*). These seats are made of wood, with carved foliage, and inlaid with mother of pearl and tortoise-shell, but in St Lazarus is a very ancient throne, transported there from another church; many foreign visitors have remarked on the perfection of its carving, but it is in no wise esteemed by the Greeks, who have lost all taste and all notion of the beautiful.

Outside the church is the cemetery of Protestant strangers. There are many tombs, especially of Englishmen, adorned with marble.

Not far from the church of St Lazarus the Turks have a small modern mosque. And near it is a bath open to persons of all classes.

The drinking water of the town is most excellent. It comes from an abundant spring in the village of Arpera, which is divided just outside Larnaca, part of it supplying that town. The aqueducts, which are carried on stone arches of good construction, are the work of the last Pasha who ruled the island, and are still kept in good order, a duty which the inhabitants of the district owe to the said Pasha, who not only helped them with the plan and its execution, but also left them a certain income, for the repair of the aqueducts when they might threaten to fall or had actually fallen. His wishes are most faithfully observed, for the matter is one of universal interest.

The command of the town of the Salines rests with the Commissioner of Larnaca, who is represented by the Chief Officer of Customs; there is also a Harbour Master (*iskele-aghasi*) whose duty is to watch so much of the coast as is under this custom-house, to prevent fraud in the exportation and importation of merchandise.

As the roadstead of the Salines is the place where not only

merchant vessels but the ships of war of all sovereigns anchor, I have thought it well to give an account of what takes place on their arrival, during their stay, and at their departure, showing the ceremonial to be observed, and the compliments to be paid to them, for ignorance on these points is a cause of inconvenience to merchantmen, and often even to the consuls.

Every war vessel then of the Christian sovereigns is saluted, just as it is on the point of dropping anchor, by all the merchantmen of every Christian European Power, to which it replies with so many guns as the rules of its own navy prescribe. It anchors and waits the salute of the Turkish fort, which cannot be fired without the order (*buyuruldu*) of the Governor of Nicosia—a messenger is sent to obtain this order, as it lies with the Governor to grant it or refuse it. Very often the consuls being warned of the arrival of a warship of their several sovereigns, obtain the *buyuruldu* beforehand, and immediately the ship comes in it is saluted by the fort, and replies with the same number of guns. The masters of the ships of the same nation are obliged, after having saluted, to go in person to report themselves to the captain. Meanwhile the consul causes notice to be given through his dragoman to his fellow consuls of the arrival of such and such a man of war, and they hoist the flags of their several consulates, while he goes with all his staff and fellow countrymen to congratulate the captain on his happy arrival.

Upon going on board a vessel whose captain has any official rank or title a consul carries his flag on the prow of his boat, a distinction which is not used in Christian ports, but is necessary here to make a show before the Turks, to give the consuls a greater importance, and to exact for them greater respect. They are received on board with sundry guns, and the same compliment is paid them on their return to the shore. If the captain desires to land, he is received on the first occasion at the landing place by all his countrymen, the consul himself, and the officials of the other consulates, who accompany him to the house in which he is to stay, generally the consular residence. While the captain is leaving his ship for the shore he receives a salute from his own vessel, and on the first occasion, from all the other vessels of his nation, while other ships hoist an ensign just as a compliment.

When a merchant ship of the same sovereign wishes to sail, besides taking its papers from the consul, permission must also be asked from the captain of the man of war, without this it cannot leave the port.

On the arrival of a Turkish war vessel the consuls immediately hoist their flags. All European vessels do the same, and fire salutes of several guns, to which the Turk replies with one gun. The masters are then obliged to wait upon the Turkish captain and inform him concerning their destination and cargo. The consuls send their dragomans on board, accompanied by a Janissary, with messages of compliment.

The warships of Christian princes fire the same salutes, which are returned gun for gun, while an officer makes the usual complimentary visit. The fort of the Salines salutes a newly arrived Turkish vessel with sundry guns : the captain replies with more or less, as he pleases.

When a Turkish man of war (or *caravel*) is in the harbour no merchantman can leave without the permission of the Turkish captain, which is never granted on the spot without the expenditure of some sequins—a clear and simple robbery. European captains are free of this exaction if a warship of their own nation chances to be in port at the moment. They can then leave after paying the ordinary compliment of informing the Turk of their intention.

No public notice is taken of the departure of a man of war of any Power from the station—the vessels only hoist their ensigns.

The salutes and compliments exchanged between the men of war of Christian princes are regulated by the rank of the respective commanders. The French and English have a mutual arrangement excusing each other from the custom.

CHAPTER III.

OF THE ANCIENT CITY OF CITIUM,
NOW DESTROYED.

LEAVING the town of Salines and walking towards the north towards the city of Larnaca you come upon masses of ruins. One grows naturally curious to know what formerly existed on this spot, and in reading in Strabo [XIV. 6, that " after Arsinoe, a city and harbour, came another harbour Leucolla. Then C. Pedalion, whence the coast is generally indented and precipitous up to Cition, which has an enclosed harbour. Then Amathus, a city, &c."]: and seeing that Ptolemaeus, v. 14, places in this order C. Pedalion, Thronoi city and cape, C. Dades, Cition city, mouth of the river Tetios, and Amathus, it seems very likely that the ruins belong to Cition. I do not know how Stephen Lusignan came to forget them when he placed Citium on the site where there is still a village called Citti, where there are no remains whatever to show that there existed there anciently a city of any consequence. And I am strongly inclined to suppose that he was in error in relying on the name of the village, which is called not after the city of Citium, but from the promontory, still called Cape Citti.

My own opinion then would be that the ruins I noticed above are really those of the ancient Citium, and this would closely follow the description of the old geographers. I have on my side too Cav. Niebuhr, surveyor to the King of Denmark, who drew a plan [*Reisebeschreibung*, III. 22, 4to,

Hamburg, 1837] which shows clearly the enclosed port which Strabo places near ancient Citium.

I had written so far when I had the luck to light on a description of Cyprus by Ascanio Savorgnano, a Venetian gentleman [published by J. P. Reinhard in the *Beylagen* to Vol. II. of his *Geschichte des Königreichs Cypern*, pp. 33—53, 4to, Erlangen, 1768]. Speaking of the position of Salines, he writes: "in ancient times there was a city there called Citium, of which the remains are clearly visible. In this place there is no height which could be other than serviceable as the site of a citadel (a thing of little cost, if one used up part of the city ramparts, *now destroyed*) which would command the place as far as that height where there was formerly a castle, *now a windmill*. One sees a channel, showing that there was once a port there; and were this channel to be a little deepened one might create a perfectly safe harbour." This being the case those maps which took for their guide the Chorograffia of Lusignan should be corrected. [Cf. de Mas Latrie, *Notice* &c. 1847: "Le bassin que j'ai vu combler pendant mon séjour à Larnaca, mais dont on trouve le dessein dans Mariti et Drummond était certainement le port fermé (λιμὴν κλειστός) dont il est question dans Strabon."]

It is quite certain that the city of Citium was not such that its position would not be clearly marked, for it was one of the most famous in the island, and the home of Zeno, the Stoic: of another Zeno, a rhetorician or poet: Apollodorus and Apollonius, physicians: Isigonus, who wrote *On Things Incredible*: Persaeus, son of Demetrius, an illustrious Stoic.

Thothmes III, a King of Egypt of the XVIIIth Dynasty, took the city from the Assyrians, and destroyed it together with other cities in Cyprus, but he rebuilt this and the rest. Apries, the Pharaoh Hophra of Jeremiah xliv. 30, defeated the Cypriots and Phoenicians in a naval combat off Citium, B.C. 588.

We now get the guidance of Herodotus, who tells (II. 182)

that Amasis (Aahmes of the XXVIth Dynasty, B.C. 569) brought all Cyprus under his rule: "he first of men took Cyprus, reducing it to pay tribute." About B.C. 525 Cambyses, son of Cyrus, having received the voluntary submission of the Phoenicians, accepted also that of the Cypriots, who then marched against Egypt (III. 19).

Cimon the Athenian, son of Miltiades, defeated a Phoenician fleet off Cyprus, and in the following year, B.C. 449, besieged Citium, and died before the town from disease, or, as some have it, from a wound.

A King of Citium, perhaps Pymatos [Pumiathon] was in favour with Alexander the Great, and gave him a sword of admirable lightness and temper, which the latter valued so well that it was always at his side, and with it he conquered Darius.

Now nothing is visible of this ancient city but the foundations of the walls which surrounded it, and of a building or two. The site is open cultivated field: and in working the soil there are found every day large stones, which are used in the modern buildings of the town of Salines and city of Larnaca.

I myself in the year 1767 happened to see an excavation made for the purpose of getting stones, among which the workmen found a head of white marble representing Antoninus Caracalla, and near it many Greek coins of the Roman Empire, of Septimius Severus, Antoninus Caracalla, and Julia Domna, with a Greek legend, and on the reverse the temple of Paphos with the inscription **KOINON KYΠPIΩN** : some with Caracalla on one side and Geta on the other, and coins of Claudius Caesar Augustus with a Latin inscription, and on the reverse a crown of laurel within which one read **KOINON KYΠPIΩN**. The head passed into the hands of Mr Timothy Turner, consul in Cyprus for His Britannic Majesty, while some of the coins I presented to the Museum of the Etruscan Academy at Cortona.

Remains exist of ancient aqueducts, proving that even in those old days it was necessary to bring in the water from distant places, for that of the town is still not good to drink.

The city was surrounded by a wide ditch, which is now under cultivation but can be traced. On its edge are the remains of two buildings, each formed of three large stones joined together: none such are found in the neighbourhood, so that it is clear they were transported hither from certain hills ten miles away. [See "A Pre-historic Building at Salamis," *Journal of Hellenic Studies*, Vol. IV. 1883.]

CHAPTER IV.

OF THE CITY OF LARNACA.

LARNACA, of which I am now to speak, should properly be called a large village, but as it is the commercial emporium of the whole island, and ranks officially next after Nicosia, though dependent on the Governor there, it can show reason for calling itself a city, being also the seat of a Greek bishopric and the residence of the consuls of the European Powers.

This city then lies at half an hour's distance from the houses of the Salines, to the north of the city of Citium: part of the foundations of the ancient walls are included in it. We know nothing of its origin: advantage may have been taken of the nearness of the harbour, and of the materials found in the ruins of Citium.

Lusignan tells us that it was already a place of some consequence when the island, in 1570, was taken by the Turks. Here are his words: " Half a league from the Marina is a large village, which is really a town, considering its merchants and trade: the government sends a Captain, a Venetian gentleman, who is changed every two years, and has already determined to make it a free town and give it some distinction." Lusignan does not give its name, but by various travellers it is called Arnica, Larnica, Larnaca, Arnaco or Larnaco.

The city is of semicircular shape, with its diameter facing south: you can walk round it in an hour. It contains no very ancient monument, merely buildings constructed by the Christians before, or the Moslem after, the conquest. The mosque was a Latin church dedicated to the Holy Cross, a small Gothic building with a porch supported by six columns of different marbles. The vault within rests on four pillars, which form three aisles: between the pillars are set little columns with their bases and capitals, well preserved but so daubed with whitewash that one cannot see of what stone or marble they are. On the left as you leave the mosque is a minaret built on the foundations of the old bell tower. This is a kind of tower, from which the Turks call the faithful to prayer. A garden adjoins the mosque, and within the same enclosure are buried the more distinguished Turks who die in the city.

Every mosque has its *Imam*, or Curate, who is bound to attend at the mosque at the hours of prayer. He is permitted to read the Qur'an and teach the people. The *Muezzin* are officials of lower rank, whose duty is to mount the minaret and call the people to prayer. They begin their call on the south side, then turn successively to the east, north and west. They shout as loudly as they can, stopping their ears with their fingers: the call is in Arabic, and invokes the names of God and Mohammad.

The Turks are bound to pray five times a day, at the dawn, at midday, at three o'clock, at sunset, and lastly at midnight. On Friday, their day of rest, they say a sixth prayer some hours after sunrise. Busy people omit to pray at some of these hours, and observe one or two only. Before prayer they wash very carefully their hands and feet and other parts of the body, and every place where they pray, be it in the open field, they hold to be sacred. When they begin to pray they kneel on a carpet or mat, or their own garment, having first made certain genuflexions, and with the face turned to the south they begin their prayer with great composure. In a quarter of an hour or little more, it is over. They turn the face towards the south to look towards Mecca, the country of their prophet, for thence, they say, came their salvation.

I must not forget that outside the said mosque there is a column of granite on which used to stand a lion, the arms of the republic of Venice. In the garden of the *Digdaban*, or Commissioner of the city, on the square opposite the mosque, there are some columns of mottled marble which may be relics of buildings which once stood in the square.

The mosque of which I have spoken is the only Turkish place of worship in Larnaca. The Greeks have three churches, St John, their cathedral, and the residence of a prelate who bears the title of bishop of Citti, where properly he should live; but that being now reduced to a mere village he lives here with his train. The next in rank is that of our Lady, called Crusopolitisa, where they preserve an ancient picture of the Virgin; the third is St Saviour. These they hold without hindrance, and each is served by a Greek priest called κοσμικὸς ἱερεύς; the inhabitants of both sexes assemble there three hours before dawn, at daybreak they must have completed all the ceremonies and celebrated the single mass which is said in each church.

The Fathers of Terra Santa have a church called St Maria di Larnaca. It is divided into three aisles, but each being shut off from the other they form three different chapels. In the middle one is a touching picture of the Virgin Mary: that on the right is set apart for women, who throughout the East, even among Catholics, are divided from the men: a custom only maintained in churches of the Latin rite on account of the prejudices of orientals. The chapel on the left, dedicated to St Francis, is used as a choir for the monks, where we may note a fine organ, the gift of the Emperor Leopold. St Maria is the parish church of the whole European colony in Larnaca, and here they are bound to fulfil the well defined duties of Catholic Christians.

In the convent are two large dormitories, and a refectory, with two good paintings by an unknown but skilful hand, one represents our Saviour washing the Apostles' feet, the other the

Marriage at Cana of Galilee. Their dispensary, fully furnished
with drugs, is worthy of remark, as well as their excellent
library, their orchards and gardens. The convent serves as
a resthouse for pilgrims on their way to and from the Holy
Places. The number of religious does not usually exceed six:
a Guardian; two Curates, one French and one Italian, the
latter must know also Greek to be able to help the Maronites
and other orientals of the Catholic communion; the dispenser,
who acts as physician and surgeon; and two other priests.
But when the pilgrims are passing through there are sometimes
as many as thirty or forty monks.

The Capucin fathers of the province of Flanders have also
a hospice[1].

Their church[1] is the private chapel of the French consul,
and several times a year he must be present there with his
colony: not however at Easter, when he must fulfil his religious
duties in the parish church of St Mary. There are generally
only three monks attached to the church, one of whom is
expected to keep a school for the children of European families,
where they learn to be good, and are taught Latin and French.
The church is small, the cells few: but they have other rooms
where they receive travelling laymen, who coming from Europe
touch at Cyprus—they admit such also to their refectory for a
daily payment of 20 paras, about 20 crazie. They live solely

---

[1] No trace of these existed in 1878, but on January 5, 1900, in digging
out stone from the wall opposite Ant. Vondiziano's house (once the consulate of Great Britain and of Russia) a stone was found rudely inscribed

✠   21 Jun.

Ann. D.   1702
D. O. M.
D.D. Fr^cus Luce Consi^rius ac
Consul Regis Galliae Hujus
Ecclesiae Primum Lapidem
apposuit Quem Benedixit R.
P. Marcus Bituricus Sup^r
Cap^rum necnon Capel^nus

on charity: the French consul sends them yearly about
15 Tuscan crowns.

It is worth noting that all the churches, Greek and Latin,
stand in a walled enclosure. In the Greek churches one enters
this kind of cloister through one or more doors just two *braccia*
high and one and a half wide, purposely built so low that the
Turks might not be able to bring in their horses or other
animals. You see the same practice throughout Syria even in
the Latin churches, but in Cyprus the gates of these enclosures
can be high and wide, for there is no fear of any intrusion on
the part of the Turks.

Churches, convents, hospices and mosques are all built
of stone. But houses and stores have for a *braccio's* depth
of foundation, and two *braccia* above the ground level courses
of stone laid in gypsum. The rest is built of bricks, made of
earth taken anywhere and mixed with water and chopped
straw. They are made in forms as in Italy, a *braccio* long
and half a *braccio* wide: they are not burned but left to dry
in the sun just where made. The same earth mixed with
straw and used fresh is used to bind them together. This
mode of building prevails throughout the island, except in the
few villages which have stone handy, but they use the same
mortar. Without the houses take a melancholy look from the
colour of the earth, but within they are airy and comfortable,
and plastered with the whitest possible gypsum, which is found
abundantly in the hills near Larnaca. They are rarely more
than two stories high, a ground and first floor: the roofs are
made of earth mixed with clay, which during the winter rains
plugs up the fissures caused by the summer heat. These roofs
are half a *braccio* thick, supported by stout beams, with cross
rafters and a double reed mat. But if the rains are long and
continuous the inmates are obliged to make frequent repairs.
However houses so built and roofed resist the shock of earth-
quakes, which stone houses do not, as quite recent experience
has taught the Cypriots. The floors are paved with a very soft

white marble, which flakes off very readily, this too a product of the island. The windows are all glazed, and every house has its own garden.

The largest houses in Larnaca, which for their size and good condition deserve to be called palaces, are these: that of Mr Tredues, who was English consul, now in the possession of MM. Pory, of French origin, where there is a hall capable of receiving comfortably 500 persons; it is adorned with ancient tapestries and pictures by good painters. The other apartments also are distinguished by equal good taste and proportions. It has stabling for 50 horses, and a most charming garden. The house inhabited by the French consul belongs to Terra Santa. This too has its merits, as well as those of the English consul, Sr Saraf, a Tuscan merchant, M. Saint Amand and M. Montagne, French merchants: that of the Venetian consul is worth a glance, and among private houses that of Sr Zambelli, a Venetian merchant, which is not yet finished, but whose cost will eventually reach 12,000 Florentine crowns.

Consuls in Cyprus hoist over the consular houses the flags of their several sovereigns on all church feasts of obligation, on those of the patron saint and birthday of each prince, on the arrival of vessels carrying the same flag, of war vessels of the Grand Signor or other sovereigns, as well as on occasions when they pay official visits to the local authorities, or to their European colleagues. The same formality is observed on the death of a consul, officer or merchant, when the ensign is kept at halfmast until the funeral is over; and lastly during a riot, to protect from outrage the premises over which the flag flies. Besides their flags consuls can put up the arms of their sovereigns over the doors of their houses; some however prefer to set them in a reception room, so as not to expose them to chance insult.

There are both Greeks and Turks who own fine and spacious houses, though not such as need particular mention, for they are of a wholly different and irregular style.

Larnaca formerly was much straitened for want of good water, the old conduits of Citium were ruinous and never repaired. But now, as I said in my account of Salines, since the water of Arpera has been brought to various fountains in the town by new aqueducts, it is most excellent.

Larnaca is governed by a *Digdaban* or Commissioner, appointed by the Governor of the island, after whom he is next in rank. His officers are the *Sirdar*, or captain of police, with the *Su-bashi* or corporals, and a very small personal staff. Here is the Court of Justice, the seat of the *Qazi* and *Khoja-bashi*, persons of good life and advanced age, whose advice is loyally received and followed. Their court can give no final decision except in matters of small moment. In grave cases a statement is drawn up and sent to the Supreme Court at Nicosia, which issues its judgment thereon.

Three hours after sunset every night a patrol of several men called *Qol-aghas* starts from the *Digdaban's* house, to prevent disorders in the town. Everyone found abroad after that hour without a light or lantern is arrested, but natives are lodged in the public prison, Europeans in the houses of their several consuls. If there is no other charge against them they are released on giving a gratuity to the guard.

In the town of Larnaca and the island generally there are colonies of six European nations, England, France, Naples, Tuscany, Venice and Ragusa, with their several consuls, except that Tuscan subjects are under the protection of the English consul, as Tuscan vice-consul. There used to be also Austrians, Danes, Swedes, Dutch and Genoese, who came recommended to one of the consuls above named, but it is a long while since they did any business there in person, their commissions being now addressed to business houses of other nationalities already established there.

Outside the town there are found in all directions under-ground large cisterns lined with so durable a glaze that they are still fit to hold oil; they were made, it is said, for this very purpose, when the island abounded in this product. It is supposed that the glaze was made with sea sand and lime mixed in boiling oil: if it be so, the island must indeed have produced olives abundantly.

Towards the western end of the town at a distance of 100 paces from the last houses there is a property belonging to the MM. Pory, a French family long domiciled in Cyprus: in one of the fields was found a subterranean chamber, full of figurines and terra cotta lamps only, so it is supposed to have been a shop where such things were made. The Turkish government forbids excavations, and MM. Pory, fearing that they could not without risk allow the search which curious persons were making there, had the shop again filled up with earth, and its position is now unknown to all but a few who are well acquainted with the place.

In 1766 Sr Zambelli, a Venetian merchant, in opening the foundations for the house which he was building to the north of Larnaca on rising ground just outside the town, found many tombs of soft marble, large enough to hold a body at full length. They bore no inscriptions, but in some were several skulls, and round them little vases of terra cotta, full of such small bones that one might think they were those of birds. The Turks affected to have a claim upon Sr Zambelli as though he had disturbed the bodies of deceased Moslem here buried, but they were made to see that the tombs were much older than their time, and that the bodies in them were not arranged in their fashion, so they held their peace, finding that they could not exact money, as they were probably prepared to do had their suspicions been verified.

To the north-west of Larnaca, a few paces outside the town there is a small mosque called by the Moslem "Arab," and by the Greeks "St Arab": both sects hold it in great veneration, the one deeming it dedicated to one of their Dervishes, the other to some saint. The Turks respect the mosque, or rather little chapel which they say was built by the said Arab, and the Greeks devoutly visit the sepulchre, a subterranean grotto in which they hold that for many years lay the body of their supposed holy hermit.

Now that we have mentioned the Dervishes it is well to say that they are a kind of Turkish monk, as are also their Santons and Abdali. The Dervishes wear a coarse woollen garment of various colours, quite open at the breast, and over it an Abba, or cloak of fine white wool which they bind in at the waist in different ways. On their heads they have a large cap of white felt, of sugar loaf shape, with a strip of the same stuff twisted round it. They wear no shirt, but they are nevertheless neat and clean, and their manners very courteous. They are commonly given to unnatural vice, and their feigned devoutness helps them to indulge their unhallowed tastes. They recognise as their founder a certain Molla Khunkiar, under whose rule they are formed into sundry convents and mosques. They preach in these twice a week, and admit to their sermons men and women, a thing not usually allowed in other mosques. One of them begins his discourse with a passage from the Qur'an, generally in condemnation of the very vices from which they themselves never abstain. The other Dervishes stand listening, separated from the people by a grating. When the sermon is over some of them begin to sing a hymn, accompanied by the music of reed-flutes, and by a dance which their chief begins and the others join in. They begin to turn very gently round the mosque, one after another, gradually increasing the pace until they circle round close together with such speed that the eye can scarcely follow them. The dance over they squat down on their heels, and wait very demurely until their chief begins the dance anew, when all follow him. This function lasts an hour and a half.

Although some persons not well versed in the subject confound Dervishes and Santons, there is a great difference between them in their dress, habits and worship. The Santons who called Hazreti Mevlana their founder, dress like Dervishes, but they are dirty, always untidy, often half naked, sometimes wholly so: their appearance is revolting, their manners very coarse and rude. Their religious exercises take place three hours after sunset, and consist in whirlings and contortions and howls which become bestial bellowings, terrible to hear. One of them meanwhile clashes cymbals or beats a drum, shouting continually Allah (God): at last they fall faint from fatigue, and foam fearfully at the mouth: it is now that Mohammadans believe that the Santons are conversing with God and Mohammad. Recovered from their swoon they feast and consort with youths and women after a most unseemly fashion. These monks however enjoy no great credit with their fellow Mohammadans. Their convents are chiefly in Anatolia.

The third order of monks, the Abdali, have no convents, but wander over Asia from one city to another, as they find more or less sympathy with their manner of life, which is much the same as that of the Santons; with this difference, that the Abdali are visited with great devotion by women, who have such faith in them that even in the public streets and markets they yield themselves to their lusts, merely taking care to cover both parties with a large cloth. In many parts of Syria such monstrous indecency is forbidden, but in Cairo they are frequently guilty of it. This may give the reader some small idea of these Turkish monks.

To return to Larnaca: about a mile to the north-west of the city is a small church dedicated to St George, which is called the little St George to distinguish it from another and large church, with the same dedication, a mile to the west of it, which is one of the most ancient in the diocese of Citium. In these churches a Papas or Greek priest officiates on feast-days only, when Mass is said there. They are adorned with various pictures, painted on the walls and on panels; there is nothing else remarkable about them.

Throughout the island and kingdom of Cyprus there is no part so bare of trees as the neighbourhood of Larnaca. There

are a few mulberry trees and palms, but the country is entirely
barren from the lack of springs of fresh water, and the abundance of stones.   Barley however grows well there.   Its orchards,
into which sweet water is brought in channels, are full of grass,
and the gardens, for the same reason, of flowers, oranges and
lemons.

CHAPTER V.

EXCURSION FROM THE CITY OF LARNACA
TO THAT OF NICOSIA.

TRAVELLING northwards from Larnaca to Nicosia the road
leaves on the right, about a mile and a half from Larnaca, a
large village, formerly called Tridato, now Livadia. The latter
name was probably taken from the fields around it. On the
west these were of some extent, then they became marshes,
but now they are drained again and partly cultivated. It is
sad to see the place so neglected; there are now hardly ten
families where 50 years ago were 2000 souls, who tilled the
ground and drew from it abundance of cotton. Silk too, the
best in the island, was produced in large quantities. Now
many of their fields lie barren; some grain is grown, little
cotton, and they have neglected altogether the cultivation of
the mulberry tree. There were whole groves of these which
the villagers keep cutting down with impunity, and without
remonstrance from the island government. There were country
houses here, whither, when the island was more flourishing, the
well-to-do people of Larnaca resorted for a change : the best of
them left belongs to MM. Pory, of whom I have spoken before,
the rest are abandoned and in ruins. There is a Greek church
dedicated to San Parascevghi.

Further on the road lies Aradippo, the richest village in the
neighbourhood. It has a Greek church dedicated to St Luke,
and every year on the feast of the saint the Greek Cypriots
hold a large fair there. There are ruins of another and older
church which was painted in fresco. The villagers here have

an exclusive right to keep pigs : in other places however the
prohibition is not strictly observed.

Two hours and a half later you reach, in the middle of a
broad plain, the village Athene. This too has a Greek church,
and its convenient situation on the road from Larnaca to the
capital keeps it a populous place, for all muleteers and travellers
make it their halting place. The country round grows corn
and oats, with clumps of mulberry trees. Leaving Athene you
see on the left two villages, one Petrofani which is inhabited
and cultivated, the other Pallio-Canuti now ruined. On the
same side lies the village of St George, and on the right Margo,
where the land is fertile but neglected. The next village, Piroi,
is well tilled; its mulberry trees and cotton fields reap the
benefit of a neighbouring torrent. You cross this, and along
a long stretch of road you find red jasper and agate mixed with
common stones. Then on the left follow three villages not far
from one another, Aghia Parascevghi, Alagichieri and Aglangià,
all inhabited and cultivated. Others, which I need not specify,
are seen in the distance. They generally show Greek churches,
and the usual clumps of mulberry trees, but the trees are fewer
than they were of old.

The mulberry trees in Cyprus are planted, as in Syria, in
regular order, and at equal distances one from the other, so as
to make a square grove composed of two, three and even five
thousand trees. The *crown* is kept at a little more than three
braccia from the ground, and the circumference at a *braccio* and a
half. They have no chance of growing taller, because every year
when they gather the leaves for their silk worms they cut the
branches. Nor do they allow them to get old, and to allow of
their being cut down when their leaves begin to fail, they take
early care to plant between them other small shoots, to take
the place of the trees that grow weak. All the care they need
is to be watered daily in summer, and to this end they lead
channels between the rows, whence the water flows into hollows
dug round each tree.

CHAPTER VI.

CONCERNING THE CITY OF NICOSIA, CAPITAL OF THE ISLAND AND KINGDOM OF CYPRUS.

TWENTY-FIVE miles to the north of Larnaca lies the city of Nicosia, which I visited in 1767, when I made the tour of the island. Its oldest recorded name is Letra, and after its restoration by Leucon, son of the first Ptolemy of Egypt, it was called Leucoton. Now the Greeks call it Lefcosia, the Italians Nicosia, and under this latter name I shall describe it. I ought however first to warn the reader that in some maps of Cyprus Nicosia is marked "*Olim Thremitus*"; a manifest error, for it was never known to history by that name. But there is a large village 12 miles to the west of Nicosia still called Thremitus, which was a city in the days of Richard, King of England, who destroyed it.

Nicosia is set in the middle of a vast plain almost in the centre of the island: mountains and hills surround it on all sides at a distance of ten miles. From the time of Constantine the Great to 1567 its circumference was nine miles. The Venetians to make it more compact and easier of defence, reduced it to three, and rounded it off with eleven bastions and three gates. The other two-thirds of the city they levelled to the ground, sparing neither churches nor palaces, the foundations of some being still in many places to be seen; particularly those of a citadel which was built by Jacques I of Lusignan, and of the convent and church of St Dominic, in which were buried several Kings, among them being Hugues IV, to whom our Boccaccio dedicated his work *De Genealogia Deorum.*

Through the middle of the ancient city flowed a stream called the Pedicus, which discharged itself near Famagusta: in the same year 1567, it was cut off therefrom, and its course diverted. But in our days it has no water, the little which it collects in the winter months being spread over the neighbouring country.

Under the House of Lusignan Nicosia was the royal residence, and an Archiepiscopal see; it contained many convents of monks and nuns, and as many as 300 churches of the Latin and Greek rites, many palaces and public buildings. Amongst its illustrious bishops was Triphyllius, about A.D. 328, of whom St Jerome wrote in his book *De Viris illustribus*, cap. XCII.: "Triphyllius, bishop of Ledra or Leucotheon in Cyprus, enjoyed great distinction in the reign of Constantius as the most eloquent man of his age. I have read his commentaries on the Song of Songs, and he is said to have composed many other works, of which none have come down to us."

At the beginning of the Lusignan rule, about 1212, Nicosia was erected into a Latin Archbishopric, by Innocent III, at the prayer of Alice, wife of Hugues I, King of Cyprus. The Blessed Hugo, our Tuscan fellow countryman, was one of the Latin bishops of Nicosia. He founded in 1268, in Calci outside Pisa, a convent of Regular Canons of St Augustine, who were thereafter called Nicosia Fathers, from the Metropolis of their founder; a fuller account will be found in the *Historia Clericorum Canonicorum* of Gabriello Penolto, L. II. C. 20. Pope Alexander IV made the Archbishop a Legate *ex officio*, with the right of wearing the robes of a cardinal, except the hat. Pius IV about 1560 left the election of the Archbishop to the republic of Venice, the Venetians choosing four persons, one of whom was appointed by the Pope.

In the fifteenth century the city, and a large part of the kingdom, fell into the hands of the Saracens, who carried off the King a prisoner to Egypt. His liberty and his crown were afterwards restored to him, but he remained a tributary. When the Sultan was overcome by the House of Othman, the Kings of Cyprus were compelled to pay to the Turks the tribute which they had paid to the Sultan, and they did so until 1570, when the island was wrested from the Venetians.

The year 1570 was fatal to Nicosia, and shortly after to the whole island. Selim II, then Sultan of the Ottomans, determined on the conquest of Cyprus. In June of that year, as we learn from the Cypriot Angelo Calepio, the island was invaded by 100,000 men, with 10,000 horses. Mustafa Pasha, the general in command, after destroying all the villages around the city, on July 26 led his army up to the walls. After a siege of 45 days, and 15 different attacks borne bravely by the besieged, at the last general assault on Saturday, September 9, Nicosia fell before the Turks. 56,000 persons were in the unhappy city, of whom 20,000 died, the others fell as slaves to the Infidels.

If you approach the city from the southern side of the island, you enter it by the Julian, now called the Famagusta, gate. Of the three gates which break the circuit of its walls this is the finest in plan and execution. A few years since one could not enter the city on horseback; now Europeans may do so, but Greek Christians must either alight or pay some small coin to the guard on duty. Within, on the side walls there are some coats of arms; among them I saw one with a cross, a rare thing in countries conquered by the Turks, who have everywhere effaced this sign.

As you walk round the ramparts you see many pieces of artillery bearing the arms of Venice. When the city was taken there were 250 cannon: the Turks brought a few more, and cast others out of the bells of the churches. They are strewn about in disorder, dismounted, some pieces spiked, others made useless, some few, bigger than the rest, were blown to pieces, and it was told me that this was done by the Pasha's orders because during the siege his camp had been most damaged by these same guns. Continuing the round of the walls you come upon two other gates, that of St Dominic, now called the Paphos gate, and that of the Provveditore, the Cerines gate. They are not as fine as the Famagusta gate, for they were never finished. The ditches round the city were not entirely dug out, nor the revetment of the wall completed, when the host of Selim began the siege. Between the Famagusta and Paphos gates, on a bastion in which Suleiman, the present Governor of Cyprus, has made a garden, there are several tombs. One more beautiful than the rest, of fine marbles, is said to cover the grave of the man who first planted the banner of Othman on the walls, the city was attacked several times at this point.

From the walls one sees scattered over the country round the city several villages and hamlets. The nearest are Caimachli, Pano-Caimachli, Palluriotissa, which was within the older circuit; St Marina, whence the fiercest bombardment was made; St Veneranda, where there was also a battery; St Demetri, in which were camped the cavalry of Mustafa Pasha; Tracone and Altalassa. Their nearness to the capital make them the most populous and best cultivated of the island. The inhabitants not only till the ground but spin cotton and weave cloth for sale in Nicosia.

Among the buildings the chief is St Sofia. This was the Cathedral church, in which the Kings of Cyprus were crowned. The plan comprises three great aisles, the style is Gothic. It contains many sepulchral stones of the house of Lusignan, and of other old Cypriots and noble Venetians: most of them are illegible, the letters being worn away, and some tombs which contained a body laid at length have been ill-used, so that the design cannot be recognised. I had an opportunity of seeing all this through the iron gratings where a small gift to the keeper allowed me to stand at my ease.

The choir, as it stood when it was used for Christian worship, together with all the altars, were destroyed when the city was taken, the church being destined to be the principal mosque, and first profaned by Mustafa Pasha who went there on September 15, 1570, to say his prayers. The outside of the fabric has suffered no change, except that the bell towers have been from the middle upwards completed in a different fashion, and most of the coats of arms of Christian families which adorned the walls have been defaced. I happened to find myself at this spot about noon on a Friday just as the Governor of the island was going to prayer. He arrived on horseback accompanied by four or five principal Turks, and all his court on foot.

Quite close to the said mosque there is another beautiful building which was dedicated to St Nicholas, bishop, as one sees from a figure of the said saint in bas-relief still remaining over the door. This church also had three aisles, and columns on which are painted various saints, much damaged. The place is now called Bezesten, a kind of market, where all kinds of goods are sold. It is the business resort of the chief merchants of Nicosia, Turks, Greeks and Armenians. If this church has not been profaned by being made a mosque, it has had no better fate in becoming a fair. Two hundred paces away stands on an open place the church of St Catherine, which was once a convent of nuns, now a mosque. The convent covered much ground, the church is rather beautiful than large.

The palace of the *Muhassil* or Governor of the island is called the Serai. Over the gate is boldly carved in stone a lion, the arms of Venice. Within is a spacious courtyard, with apartments round it and stables below. The building is Gothic and was the palace in the time of the Christian Kings, but the place has undergone so many changes at the caprice of successive Pashas and Governors that nothing remains to call for notice. In the adjoining square is a fountain of Turkish work, supplied, like all those in the city, with excellent water.

The Bazar or market is spacious and well found in food

stuffs, but it is anything but clean.   In the middle of it is
a khan, or vast courtyard, round which are many rooms: the
gate is of marble, built up of ancient remains.   This khan was
built for the benefit of foreigners generally by Muzaffer Pasha,
who imposed to this end a tax of two paras (about two crazie)
on every Cypriot.   The impost was small indeed but unjust,
and, although he had the merit of having been with Mustafa
Pasha at the taking of Nicosia, he was beheaded.   He would
not have been so punished in our days.   The place is known
as the khan of the Alajotes, because it is chiefly used by traders
from Alaja in Caramania.

The Greek Archbishop lives in a palace built up out of the
ruins of the former one.   There is nothing which particularly
deserves notice, except the cathedral church, a modern building
constructed within the palace grounds, well arranged and orna-
mented.

The Latins have two convents in Nicosia, one of the
Spanish branch of the Fathers of Terra Santa, the other of
French Capucins, who know the language of the country and
minister to the Maronite Christians.   There are no European
Catholics in the city; by Europeans meaning always subjects
of the Christian princes of Europe, called also Franks.

The Armenians, who are separated from the Catholic
church, have a bishop and a small church, as they are the
richest section of the inhabitants.

There are remains of other ancient structures only useful
as showing what the city once was.   The streets were wide
enough to set off the palaces and buildings which adorned
them, but in many places they are altered, and new houses
built of unburnt bricks have been foisted in, breaking the
regular line, and making a poor figure.

I have already mentioned Nicosia, the seat of government,
and residence of the *Muhassil* and his court, and of the *Molla*
who is chief of the judges or *Qazis* of the island: I need only
add that it is the ordinary residence of all the *aghas* or Turkish

gentlemen, and of the principal Greek and Armenian families, members of which occupy various posts in the central government.

There is some trade here in cotton fabrics, some of them made in the city, but most in the villages outside. They have the art of dying in red and yellow skins tanned with sumach, and the general opinion is that the colours are brighter than those of Barbary. They stamp cotton cloths with indelible colours, which get prettier with washing. They dye also the red cloth called *bucassini*, for which they use the root madder or alizari, a product of the island, mixed with ox-blood; this colour too is durable and never fades. Other island produce is collected in Nicosia, together with imports from Caramania, but they all find their way to the traders of Larnaca whence they are distributed.

While at Nicosia I found myself at several Turkish entertainments, particularly at the circumcision of four little boys, and at the wedding of a Turkish gentleman. I shall do well to give some account of them here.

Circumcision among the Turks is performed after the completion of the boy's seventh year: but at a child's birth a little salt is put in its mouth, with some words from the Qur'an to the effect "precious to thee for the gift of life be the name of the true God, to Whom thou shalt give honour and glory." For eight days before they get up feasting and merry-makings, then, on the appointed day, the boy is clothed in gala dress, and led through the city on a horse with gay trappings. The green banner of Islam precedes him, and *singis* or dancers. Followed by various instruments and the crowd, he is conducted to a mosque, where prayer is said, and then to his home, where an expert performs the operation, while the patient repeats their confession of faith, lifting the thumb, and using the words "*La ilaha illa Allah, wa Mohammad rasul Allah*"—there is no god but God, and Mohammad is His prophet. The function over the guests make presents to the

new Muslim, and the festival ends with a sumptuous dinner.
Women make a simple confession of faith, as above.

As I am going to speak of the marriage of Turks, let me say
something first of their loves. It is quite clear that Turkish
men cannot indulge in amorous converse with women, the
latter being always well guarded in their houses, and not even
when they are betrothed are the lovers allowed to meet, or to
see each other before the wedding day. They contrive however to make a lively and even extravagant show of their
passion. They often pass under the windows of the loved
one, singing songs, and brandishing an unsheathed khanjar or
knife. Then they put the point to their arms or breast, drive
it into the flesh, and as they draw it out enlarge the wound.
If the lady does not notice these affectionate demonstrations
her lover is satisfied with being able to show her later the
scars. Even the Greeks, who have copied many of the Turkish
customs, are guilty sometimes of like childishness. What the
women do is unseen.

Turks can take wives of three kinds, with whom they may
consort; legitimate wives, whom they marry; *Kebin*, whom they
hire; and slaves, whom they buy.

The legitimate wives whom they must marry, and cannot
see until they do marry, may be four in number, whom they
may have at one time, and in the same house. The Qazi, who
acts on these occasions as notary, registers the contract of
marriage. One of its chief and invariable conditions is the
assignment to the bride of a dowry, although the portion she
brings her husband be little or nothing. After this the bridegroom goes on horseback, accompanied by a festive crowd of
relations and friends, to pray in the mosque, where the Imam
confirms the contract with his blessing. When these acts,
which are considered of Divine obligation, are completed the
bride is led to the bridegroom's house, covered with a veil.
On his return from the mosque he removes this veil, in token
that so he will remove the reproach of her sex, and then leaves

her to amuse herself and feast with the other women while he does the same with the men, and at last all retire to their own apartment.

For a woman married by *Kebin*, or hire, there are fewer formalities. A contract is made before the judge, specifying the time for which the man wishes to keep her; the sum, as agreed upon between the parties, to be paid by the man, and a condition that he shall maintain the issue of the marriage, the children being considered legitimate and capable of inheriting.

Of slaves they may have as many as they can keep, and they avail themselves of this right without any further formality than that of purchase. The father must maintain the children of such unions, but if at his death he does not allot them a share in his property they have no claim on it, and remain at the mercy of the legitimate heirs.

A Turk who is tired of a legitimate wife can, without giving a reason, divorce her: but then he must pay the woman the dowry assigned to her in the marriage contract, and restore to her the property she brought to his house. If he has an adequate reason for separating from her, he is not obliged to give her anything; but in both cases the children remain at the husband's charge. The woman cannot marry again until she has been divorced four months, to see if she is *enceinte*: if she is, she must wait the birth of the child, which remains with the father. If after the divorce the parties wish to live together again, the woman must first marry another man, who does not care to keep her; they are then free to remarry. When a reconciliation of this sort is to be effected, the man tries to find a friend to play the part of the new husband, with whom he agrees for the restoration of the woman.

A Turkish woman cannot, like a man, obtain a divorce without reason given. But she is entitled to demand it when her husband does not give her sufficient food: if he does not admit her to his bed at least once in eight days, and if he does not give her money to go to the bath. In these cases the man is obliged to release her, to restore her dowry, and to maintain all the children.

The woman can also claim a divorce if her husband is addicted to unnatural vice. To ask a dissolution of marriage on this plea she goes to the judge, and without further explanation she takes off a boot or slipper, and lays it before him up-side-down. A husband so charged is taken, beaten on the soles of his feet, and separated forthwith from his wife, without getting a chance of excusing himself.

Slaves cannot demand a divorce; only if they do not get sufficient food they can claim to be sold to another Turk.

Although the Turks may have different forms of marriage, yet, speaking generally, women throughout the Levant are but slaves. The reasons are many: I will end this chapter with one set down in the words of the famous Montesquieu. He is speaking of southern women, but his statement applies perfectly to those of the Levant.

"Women in hot climates are marriageable at eight, nine and ten years of age, and infancy and wedlock are generally but one state. They are old at 20, so that they never display at one time reason and beauty. When beauty claims influence, reason causes it to be refused: when reason might obtain it, beauty has vanished.

"Women must always be in a state of dependence, for reason cannot procure for them in old age an influence which even in their youth beauty had not given them." (*Esprit des Lois*, XVI. 2.)

CHAPTER VII.

EXCURSION FROM THE CITY OF NICOSIA TO THE TOWN AND FORTRESS OF CERINES.

OUTSIDE the gate by which one leaves Nicosia for Cerines, along a good stretch of road one sees many Turkish graves, some of them constructed with fine marbles and columns, fragments of buildings once existing within the city. After an hour's march across the plain you cross by two different well-built stone bridges two branches of the river or torrent Pedicus. Red jasper is found in its bed. Beyond the Pedicus lies the village of Dicomos, where there is nothing to note except a large house belonging to a Turkish *agha*, and many clumps of mulberry trees. Other villages are in sight, and the adjoining country bears cotton plants and mulberry trees.

After crossing the whole plain you reach the skirts of the northern range, which traverses the island from west to east. All the paths across it are steep and difficult, the least inconvenient is that commonly called the Boghaz (gullet): it runs between two hills, sometimes only wide enough for one person to pass, at others a cart might travel on it. Beyond the Boghaz the road mounts to its highest point, whence you see the sea of Cilicia or Caramania, and the north coast of the island. In descending on the other side you skirt a broad valley, abounding in springs. At the bottom are sundry old buildings, which they say were fortifications; they might have been attacked, but they were incapable of defence, so I prefer to think them ruined-mills, such as I have seen elsewhere. All the mountains are covered with small trees and brushwood.

CHAPTER VIII.

THE TOWN AND FORTRESS OF CERINES.

THE town and fortress of Cerines are about 20 miles distant from Nicosia. The town is thinly peopled. The schismatic Greeks, who make up the Christian population of the island, have a church there, the seat of a bishop, and the Turks a mosque. The government is administered by a commissioner and a judge. The inhabitants till the surrounding country, which gives a good return for their labour, for its many springs make this one of the most fertile districts in Cyprus. It produces wheat, barley, silk, cotton, oil and carobs; of these last whole shiploads are sent every year to Alexandria.

Cerines was already a city in the days of the Orthodox Greek bishops, among whom was St Theodotus, of whom Caesar Baronius in the Roman Martyrology, May 6, writes: "In Cyprus St Theodotus, bishop of Cyrenia, who suffered cruel torments under the Emperor Licinius, died when peace was restored to the Church." [H. Delehaye, *SS. de Chypre*, 258.]

Cerines, says Lusignan, was built by Cyrus, King of Persia, after he had subdued the nine Kings of Cyprus. That he conquered the Cypriots we know from Xenophon, XVI. 2, who writes: "after marching down to the sea he brought under his sway the Cypriots and Egyptians." However that may be, ruins exist about the town, and part of the old walls, which are certainly not later than the Roman era. On the west are many grottos the entrances to which are made or squared with the chisel, and within are three or four niches fitted for corpses: the peasants call them the tombs of the Gentiles. Two hundred paces further are the quarries out of which were dug the stones used in building—not, I think, the ancient city, but rather—the fortress which I am about to describe.

The castle of Cerines is built on the seashore upon a rock: its foundation is clearly coeval with that of the ancient city, but it was enlarged by the Lusignan Kings. Europeans are not allowed to enter it, and the Turks look angrily at anyone who comes too near its walls. I was allowed to study them, and even to enter the ditch which surrounds them. It is one of the best preserved forts which I have seen in this part of the world in the hands of the Turks, although some few years ago it was injured in several places by cannon-shots, aimed at it by Kior Mohammad Pasha to dislodge a party of insurgents who had fortified themselves within.

To give an idea of its construction I will borrow the words of a manuscript of the sixteenth century. "The shape of this little fort is an irregular oval. There are three old fashioned towers, hollow, weak and small, in the fourth corner is a bastion, badly planned and weak. The ditch is 21 paces broad and 370 round: the walls are four paces thick on foundations of six paces, and their height over 16."

Its situation is highly unfavourable, for the hills are barely a mile and a half away. Nevertheless King Jacques, natural son of King Jean, after a siege of two years, and various assaults by the Saracens could not take it. It surrendered at last in 1462 through the treachery of Sor de Naves, who commanded its garrison in the interest of Carlotta, the legitimate heir to the crown of Cyprus.

The Queen, as we learn from Scipio Ammirato (Book XXIII. November 10, 1461), "came to Florence when Alessandro Macchiavelli was Gonfaloniere, on her way to Rome to beg the Pope's aid against Jacques, her bastard brother, who

4—2

had, with the forces of the Sultan of Cairo, unjustly occupied her Kingdom, which did not belong to him, and further held her husband, Louis of Savoy, besieged within the fortress of Nicosia. Many honours were paid to her by the Republic, and she visited the church of St Miniato, where the Cardinal of Lisbon, brother of her first husband, was interred." The Abbé Mecalti also in his *Chronological History of Florence* says that Queen Carlotta was welcomed with great honour in the house of Cosimo de' Medici, Pater Patriae.

After the fall of Nicosia in 1570 the fort of Cerines surrendered without resistance to the troops of Selim. In the time of the Venetians it had a Commandant, and a Captain with 50 soldiers: now, under the Turks, it has a *Disdar* or Commandant, without soldiers. Among the cannon which arm it, most of which bear the arms of Venice, I was told there are some fine culverins. On the sea side there are several guns planted at the sea level.

The Sultan, having a vast empire, is obliged to send Pashas to govern its various provinces, who have much the same authority as the Roman Proconsuls. But through fear that these may rebel against the Ottoman power he takes little trouble to repair the strongholds which are remote from the capital; and further, to put all idea of rising out of their heads, he keeps the forts without warlike supplies. In this very castle, where there was an ample supply of necessaries, the *Disdar*, who in 1765 put himself at the head of one party of the rebels, was able to hold out for several months. The intervention of a Pasha, with troops from the mainland, was necessary to bring him to reason. The castle is now in some places out of repair; and it is even said that the Sultan has given orders for its destruction, which have not been carried out.

Close to the fort is a harbour, or rather a basin, just large enough for two or three small vessels. It is the point of embarkation for Caramania; the passage is made in seven or eight hours.　It is a great convenience to the island to receive frequently by this route letters from Constantinople and Europe generally: two French boats are constantly employed on this service.　Other vessels which trade with this side of the island, especially for carobs, stand out to sea about three miles.　The landing is bad, and only possible in summer.　From the shore near Cerines the Caramanian mainland is visible; lights can be seen across the strait, and are used as signals to the boats, when there are passengers waiting, and both boats are on the same coast.

Just outside the town on the west is a small church, now in the hands of the Greeks, formerly in those of the Latins, dedicated to the Madonna, where is a sepulchral stone with the effigy and epitaph of the engineer who completed the fortifications of the castle.

Along the shore to the east of Cerines are the villages of Amtara and Accatu (formerly Acte Argivorum), both of them on the site of cities: and Clides, once a large village now called Cape S. Andrea.　There is nothing else worthy of notice.

CHAPTER IX.

DEPARTURE FROM CERINES, AND DESCRIPTION OF THE CONVENT OF LAPASIS.

THE road from Cerines to the monastery of Lapasis runs eastwards. You travel for five miles over the most beautiful plain in Cyprus, so well is it cultivated, so many the trees, both fruit and forest trees, and so green the little hills, which never lack water and keep their verdure all the year round. The same charms adorn all this northern coast.

By this pleasant path you reach the convent, lying under the mountains. It was an abbey of the "Umiliati," called Lapasis, now written corruptly Belapais, and by Italians Belpaese. Its natural position has well earned the name. On the slope of a hill, it enjoys the most exquisite view of mounds covered with groves and young trees, and a fair plain, stretching down to the sea. It has the same kind of view on the east and the west, covering also the Caramanian Sea and the shore of the mainland.

The abbey was built by Hugues III de Lusignan, who gave it sundry privileges, this the chief: that the Superior besides the robes of a mitred abbot, might wear in riding a sword, and the gilt spurs of a knight of the kingdom.

In the days of Jacques the bastard it was made a *Commenda*, and after the surrender of the fort of Cerines the abbey was demolished. There still remain the melancholy ruins of a vast building. You enter a glorious cloister surrounded by 18 pillars, or rather pilasters, with Corinthian capitals; on the left is a door above which are carved the arms of Lusignan. This leads to a refectory 90 feet long, and 32 broad. The vault is carried by seven columns; and on the north are six very large windows, from which there is a charming view. Between two of these windows is the pulpit, from which the monks read during meals: it is reached by a convenient stair-case constructed in the thickness of the wall. Directly opposite the entrance, under the first arch of the cloister, are two large sarcophagi of white marble of Roman work. The lower one is smooth, and used to receive the water from the one above it, which served as a *lavabo* for the refectory. This last is a single block of very white marble, long enough to receive a human body, and about two *braccia* in height. The monu-ment is surrounded with a festoon of flowers and fruits, which begins between the horns of a bull's head: at the corners it is caught up on four rams' heads, and in the middle of the front by the hands of a child, well executed in *basso relievo*. In the spaces left vacant by the curves of the festoon are lions' heads, carved in full face; of these there are six, two in each larger, one in each smaller square.

In an excavation made at Beirut among the ruins of the ancient city I saw a similar sarcophagus, so far differing from this that on the angles were four eagles, and in front a crown, from which started a similar festoon which ended behind in various knots on the head of a bull. This had a cover of triangular section, adorned with laurel leaves arranged like fishes' scales: the tomb at Lapasis had no cover.

Under the refectory is a chamber, 66 feet long and 32 broad, of roughly squared stones, with a vault upheld in the middle by only two columns. It is constructed on the slope of the hill, and gets air from the northern side and also from a huge door towards the east, but this latter is getting choked with the earth which falls from the mountain.

For all the injuries that the building has received almost unavoidably from men and time, in some parts it is well preserved, particularly so in this subterranean chamber, which seems built but yesterday. The ruins now serve as a refuge to shepherds and their flocks when surprised by rain.

The church has survived. The entrance is on the right, under the loggia, which rests on four columns. Against the wall are two arches of marble, over which is painted the shield of the house of Lusignan. In one of these, the nearest to the door of the church, was buried Hugues III, the founder of the abbey. His distinguished career won him the title of Hugues le Grand, and as such St Thomas Aquinas dedicated to him the book *de regimine Principum*. On the outer wall above the door, exposed to all weathers, are several pictures of saints. The interior of the church is now arranged for the Greek rite, with the sanctuary divided by the usual wooden screen. The vault rests on four stout columns of stone, built up of several blocks; the church, which is 70 feet long and 46 broad, is thus divided into three aisles.

At a short distance from the convent is the village of Casafani, where I found the best water I have tasted in Cyprus.

CHAPTER X.

EXCURSION FROM LAPASIS TO THE CONVENT
OF ST CHRYSOSTOM.

In going to the convent of St Chrysostom, which lies under the castle of Buffavento, the northern range is crossed by steep and difficult paths; the sea is lost to view, and the mountains run parallel with it towards the east. One passes the village of Sicorudi, which is inhabited and cultivated, and then Vunâ, otherwise called St Romano from a church dedicated to that saint. It belongs to the Maronites, who are the principal inhabitants of the village. Keeping on the same road one finds, 12 miles from Lapasis, the monastery of St Chrysostom, tenanted by Greek monks of the order of St Basil.

This monastery had its origin as far back as the days of the first Christian Emperor. I noticed that the church was of more modern workmanship, and one of the monks told me that it was built later by a noble Cypriot lady, who has also enlarged their monastery.

The church is small, with a marble pavement, and pictures in the Greek style. In the porch is a sepulchral stone over which the Greeks keep a lamp continually burning, for they say that this is the tomb of that noble lady who built the church. Near her are buried two female slaves, who were her favourites, and whom in death she wished to have near her, in gratitude for the trouble they took in helping and tending her in her last illness. Near this is another smaller church, also old, but it is no longer used for divine service or treated as a place of worship, and serves as a shelter for animals.

If the monastery is wanting in the magnificence which one sees in others in the island, still it has many conveniences, and from its site on the skirts of the mountains it enjoys a view of the plain of Nicosia, and its neighbourhood full of farms and villages which it would be long to enumerate. There are generally ten or twelve monks there: the Greeks call them *Calogeroi* and they obey an *Hegoumenos* or Superior. It is to be noted that these *Calogeroi* are all Regulars, distributed in three different orders, of St Basil, St Elias and St Marcellus. All three take the vows of poverty, chastity, and obedience; they do not eat flesh, and live a very austere life.

Few of those who go to St Chrysostom fail to visit the ruins of the ancient castle of Buffavento on the highest point of the northern range. The slopes of the mountain on which the castle stands are about two miles from St Chrysostom and are reached by a gentle ascent. Thence you see a peak which it seems impossible to scale, but at last with some risk, and climbing with feet and hands along narrow ledges, in about an hour you get to the ruins of the ancient castle, which was purposely demolished, along with several others in the island, by the Venetians. It is wonderful how men could ever have raised a building so strong and extensive, with about 100 chambers, especially if you think of the water necessary for the work; but as one sees various cisterns, one must suppose that these were built first, and that rain water was used in the construction of the castle.

This was built in the thirteenth century by a noble Cypriot lady, the very same who erected the church of St Chrysostom, and here she retired to be free from the persecutions of the Templars, who for a year or little more that they held Cyprus tyrannised over the natives. Hence they were compelled to restore the island to King Richard of England, who had sold

it to them for 100,000 ducats, and they received back their
money.

From the highest point of this castle one sees the whole
island, and the sea which surrounds it, except just where
Mt Olympus hides a small part of it.   The view is very
extensive, for in one glance, besides the various districts of
the island, are seen also the mountains on the mainland
of Caramania, and those of Syria, which I suppose must be
the range of the Lebanon.   The descent of the mountain is
as toilsome as the ascent, as it is so steep that it requires an
hour to come down.   Below are the remains of various buildings.   The Cypriots say that there was once a delightful garden
here, called Paradise.   In a little more than half an hour you
reach the monastery.

To anyone who stays there, though it may be for several
days, these kindly monks give a lodging, and provide themselves for his wants.   Repayment is only sought for what they
spent, the rest is left to the charity of their guest, who generally
leaves an alms for the church.

CHAPTER XI.

DEPARTURE FROM ST CHRYSOSTOM: ARRIVAL
AT CITEREA: DESCRIPTION OF THE VILLAGE.
DEPARTURE THENCE FOR FAMAGUSTA.

WE descend sundry barren stony hills, and five miles to
the east of St Chrysostom reach the village Citerea, which
lies under one of the peaks of the northern range, called
Pentadactylon. The story runs that the mountain takes its
name from five huge fingers of copper, which had been set on
its five peaks to ward off the strong north winds: for the
peasants believe that the metal has such power. But the
experience of the year 1767 shows that, although the fingers
are gone, the north wind has made itself very rarely felt.
Without enquiring further why these colossal fingers were so
erected, it may suffice to say that they were taken down by
Jacques the bastard, and coined into money to meet his
necessities. He did the same with all the caldrons and baths
in the island.

Citerea is made up of several villages, one close to the
other; the mulberry trees round them make quite a grove.
This is one of the most productive parts of the island; it is
especially rich in silk and cotton, and its fields are abundantly
watered by a spring on the north of the village, called Cefalo-
friso, or well-head, in which are three large jets, which throw
out so much water that a few paces only from the source it
turns a mill. There are many more mills below which grind
grain for the neighbourhood, and for the city of Nicosia,

eight miles away. In old time this water was carried as far as Salamis by aqueducts, of which some remains are still visible.

The Cypriots are very fond of visiting this place for recreation, but they are scarcely fit judges of real pleasantness, so long as they think that the most beautiful spot where there is most water. Citerea really has no merits except for its produce: and let no one fancy that here was the ancient city Cythera, where was a temple of the goddess Venus, for that lay between Pafo and Limasol. The village of which I am speaking was called Citri, and now by Europeans Citera and by the Greeks Cirgà. From the spring, where the mulberry trees begin, to the plain, where they end, is about two miles.

Leaving Citerea you enter the great plain of Mesaria through the village of Palecciatro. Villages and hamlets are dotted over the plain, some inhabited, some abandoned; but the country generally is well cultivated with wheat, barley and cotton. Ruins of the aqueducts which supplied Salamis with water occur here and there, but unless one knew that they had existed there is very little by which to trace them. It is a journey of 30 miles from Citerea to the walls of Famagusta.

CHAPTER XII.

THE CITY OF FAMAGUSTA AND ITS
NEIGHBOURHOOD.

THE city of Famagusta was formerly called Arsinoe, after the sister of Ptolemy Philadelphus, its founder. Its actual name Famagusta is a corruption of Ammochostos, which means buried in the sand, from the sandy soil which surrounds it. It lies on the eastern shore of the island. As you approach the walls the city is scarcely visible, for the land outside slopes so as to hide all but a few feet of the highest buildings. It is built on a rock, with a circuit of two miles. The walls are stout and broad, sloping in at the top, and surrounded by a ditch carefully hewn out, very deep and 20 paces wide. There are twelve old fashioned towers disposed round the city, with walls four paces thick, and an inner breadth of five paces. Within there is a cavalier, three bastions, a curtain with two ranks of artillery, and a citadel. It was fortified by Guy de Lusignan in 1193: the Genoese, who held it for 90 years, strengthened it, as did also Jacques the bastard, when he got it back into his power, and lastly the Venetians.

There are two gates, each with its drawbridge; one on the land side, the other towards the sea; the latter gives access to the port, which is entered by a narrow opening, still closed every night by a chain fastened to one of the bastions of the harbour. Only empty vessels can enter, not from any defect in the entrance, which is deep, but because the harbour is nearly choked up. On the east it is guarded by a reef of rocks, which breaks the fury of the waves, and allows vessels to lie in safety.   Captains choose the place to refit and careen their ships.

In Famagusta the Lusignan Kings assumed the crown of Jerusalem until the city was taken by the Genoese, when they took it, together with that of Cyprus, in the cathedral church of Nicosia.   The Genoese gained possession of Famagusta in 1376, in the reign of Pierre II.   His successor Jacques recognised their claim to the city and a circuit of six miles round it, and this they governed according to their own laws.   In the fifteenth century, when after a siege of three years it fell into the hands of Jacques the bastard upon fair conditions of truce, one of the articles stipulated that he should still rule it by Genoese law.

About 1490, when the island came under the Venetians, Famagusta was governed by a Captain, a Venetian gentleman, who had absolute power.   In the citadel were two Commandants, and in time of peace 50 soldiers, under four superior officers.

Mustafa Pasha, General for Selim, began on July 24, 1570, by sending a detachment of 500 horsemen to cut off the supplies of the city, while he himself continued the siege of Nicosia. Upon the fall of that city he sent to demand the surrender of the town and fortress of Famagusta.   He was bidden come to their walls with all his army, to receive the hardy and haughty reply of the citizens.   Upon this Mustafa led his forces on September 18 of the same year against Famagusta, and encamped on the west, near the village Pomo d'Adamo : on the 23rd he closed round the city, and early in October began to besiege it.   In April, 1571, he drew his lines closer in, his headquarters being in the gardens just outside the town. Marc' Antonio Bragadino was Captain, and with other brave and noble gentlemen defended the place, which is the key of the realm.   There were then 8000 souls within the walls, 4000 being fit to bear arms.   After it had sustained with heroic courage six fierce assaults, at last on August 1, 1571, the city surrendered upon honourable terms, which were violated by the treacherous Mustafa.

On August 5 the Captain went fearlessly to Mustafa's tent to hand over the keys and take his leave, before sailing from the island as the convention allowed. Bragadino was accompanied by Estor Baglione, Captain-general of the forces, and other commanders and officers. The Pasha was very desirous of seeing him before he embarked, but when he came into his presence he invented, in Turkish fashion, a malicious trick, and accused Bragadino of allowing the murder of certain Turks in the city during the truce. On such a pretext he caused the said knights and lords to be slain, cut off Bragadino's ears and nose, and set him to work on the walls.

Mustafa entered Famagusta on August 7, and hanged there Tiepolo, Captain of Pafo, whom Bragadino had left to look after affairs after his departure. And finally, on August 17, after many torments borne with heroic firmness, Bragadino was savagely flayed alive. His skin was filled with straw, and the body quartered and set up on different points of the ramparts. The skin was then put in a box with the heads of Estor Baglione, Luigi Martinengo, another Bragadino, commanding in the citadel, and Quirini; all of these were sent to Constantinople and presented to the Grand Signor. The hero's skin was afterwards ransomed by Antonio, Bragadino's brother, and Marco Ermolao and Antonio his sons, who caused it to be interred in 1596 in the church of St John and St Paul at Venice.

The besieging army consisted of 200,000 men; Mustafa's own troops were 94,000, the rest were adventurers from Syria, Caramania and Anatolia. During the ten months of the siege the Turks fired 140,000 balls; very many of these are still found in the gardens and fields about Famagusta, and some are piled in the ditch. 75,000 Turks died during the siege. I have borrowed most of these military details from the account of the siege written by a contemporary, the Cypriot Angelo Calepio.

About 1370, St Bridget, then a widow, touched at Cyprus on her way to Jerusalem. The Queen-regnant was Eleonora, daughter of the Duke of Milan and widow of King Pierre I of Lusignan, who was killed by his own brothers. The saint tried to amend the evil habits of the islanders, and published a revelation from God threatening the kingdom, unless its inhabitants returned into the ways of the Lord. At the prayer of Queen Eleonora she remained for the coronation of Pierre II, who assumed in Nicosia the crown of Cyprus, and in Famagusta that of Jerusalem. After visiting the Holy Places St Bridget returned to Famagusta, where she predicted the destruction of the city and realm, which was only too soon verified. She did not leave Famagusta before she had suffered grievous persecution, as may be seen at length in her life by Father Burlamacchi, Book II, chapters 23 and 24.

So great was the wrath felt by the Turks against the Europeans in Famagusta, when they weighed all the loss caused to them by 4000 men only, that they forbad every European to enter or leave it on horseback; even now on reaching the gate they are obliged to alight.

The city has lost on the outside nothing of its original works; the ditches are thoroughly cleared, the walls in order, except that a few towers damaged by the enemy's guns remain unrepaired. It is very different within, where in every street you meet only ruin and destruction. The number of churches destroyed is immense; some people even say that within the narrow enclosure there were 200. This might be true, for I have seen four or five close together; most of them were high, but of no great size. Among them the Latin cathedral of St Nicholas, now the chief mosque, is worthy of remark. Its style is exactly that of St Sophia at Nicosia. It contains several sepulchral monuments. Jacques the bastard and his son Jacques III were buried here.

Opposite the church, on the square, are three arches resting on several columns of oriental granite, with the arms of Venice in the middle. The rest of the wall is covered with the arms of Venetian and Genoese families, who had borne rule in the city. Behind the arches is another part of the square, at the end of which are the ruins of the palace of the Commandants.

The church of St Cross, the Greek cathedral, was selected, as being one of the best buildings, for a mosque, and thus escaped the fate of the rest. That of St Paul was one of the finest, but though it was not profaned by the Turks it was unhappily abandoned, and is falling day by day into ruin. It was built by a certain merchant, Simone Nostrano, with a portion of the gains which he made in a single voyage to Syria. This was in the fourteenth century, in the days of Pierre I, when through its commerce the island flourished greatly. This same King Pierre came to Florence in 1368, where he was received by the Republic, Giovanni Sostegni being Gonfaloniere, with the honours due to so great a prince. The Greeks have still a church dedicated to St George: the Latin Christians have none, for Mustafa Pasha would not allow them to hold either churches or houses in the city. The body of St Epiphanios, bishop of Salamis, was buried in Famagusta, but I do not know what became of it after the sack of the city.

The citadel is in good repair. Criminals are confined there from Cyprus, and other parts of the Ottoman Empire, who are specially banished here, as certain great lords of Constantinople—the ditch round it, which was filled from the sea, is now mostly choked up. On the east of the city are the ruins of the arsenal, where galleys were built, and close to the northern wall the foundry for cannon: this is intact, and the implements used about the furnaces are still there. On the square, almost close to the demolished palace of the Governor, is the armoury which is still full of arms of the times of the

Christian kings, and even older still; but only a short while since it was entirely walled up, windows, doors and all, and its very memory effaced. This was to prevent arms being ready at hand in case of a popular tumult. On the walls are many cannon, some of them of great size, but all dismounted and in bad condition.

Who would believe it? So deserted is the city that it contains but 200 souls. The ancient houses are being constantly sold; men buy them to pull them down and carry off their woodwork, especially beams and rafters. But it is strictly forbidden to take away a single stone, so that everywhere you see great heaps.

The city is now governed by an *Agha* who acts also as Customs officer for the little trade carried on by sea. There is also a judge, and a Commandant with a few Janissaries. There is no trade, but as European vessels often touch here to refit, there is an agent who acts for all the European nations represented in Larnaca. He is generally a Turk, chosen for his pliancy and friendly attitude, like the present Mohammad Reis.

Outside Famagusta along the shore towards the south are gardens, full of lemon, orange and other fruit trees. Among them is the *qayssi*, a species of apricot, whose fruit has a red and white skin, of delicate flavour but little substance. It is ripe in May, and lasts scarcely more than a month. It is esteemed as being both pleasant and wholesome. The rest of the country is almost as rich in cotton plants and mulberry trees as Citerea. Near the gardens is the village Varoshia, which has several Greek churches. Returning to the city, at no great distance from the walls I noticed the church of St Mary, evidently of very ancient date. Just before this again are the aqueducts which should supply Famagusta with water, but they are so much neglected that they are often empty. As you pass the city going north you see many ruined houses and deserted gardens. I fancy they date from the time when the enemy

encamped here, as the style of the houses is very different
from that in use since the island fell into the hands of the
barbarians.

The climate in this part is by no means the best in Cyprus.
The heat is greater, because the soil is chiefly sand; and the
lake of Costanza, not far off, does not always dry up in
summer, and its exhalations infect the air. This lake has
formed since the river or torrent Pedicus, which flows here
from the neighbourhood of Nicosia, has no longer its usual
outlet to the sea between Salamina and Famagusta, as it is
marked in ancient maps.

CHAPTER XIII.

OF THE ANCIENT CITY OF SALAMINA NOW DESTROYED AND ITS NEIGHBOURHOOD.

SIX miles to the east of Famagusta lies the ancient city of Salamina, which traces its origin to Teucer, who built it after Telamon his father drove him from his home in the island of Salamis. Horace (I. *Ode* vii. 27) sings of his courage

" 'Tis Teucer leads, 'tis Teucer breathes the wind;
  No more despair; Apollo's word is true;
  Another Salamis in kindlier air
    Shall yet arise."

Evagoras was King of Cyprus, but overcome in battle by the Persians he was forced to be content with the one city of Salamina, where afterwards reigned a second Evagoras, his grandson, who was dethroned by [Pnytagoras in B.C. 350]. Under the Persians it shared the common fate of the rest of the island. King Costa, father of Catherine, virgin and martyr, also reigned there, and gave it his name Constantia. St Jerome (*In Epitaphio Paulae ad Eustochium*, vol. I. col. 693), speaks of it as "Salamina, which is now called Constantia." The Greek Christians had a bishopric there, afterwards transferred to Famagusta. Lastly it was destroyed by the Saracens in the reign of Heraclius, was then abandoned and never rebuilt.

In our day not a single building remains to give us an idea of its former greatness: a few columns scattered here and there, great heaps of stones, and fragments of an edifice which might possibly have been a temple. The oldest existing remains are the cisterns or reservoirs which stored the water brought from Citerea, for the waters of the city were never good to drink.

The city had a harbour called Port Salamino, and later Port Costanzo. Traces of it are visible, but it is ruined and choked, and only .fit for small boats.

Many illustrious men are credited to this city, Ariston, a Greek historian (mentioned by the geographer Strabo, lib. XIV.) Ṣolon, one of the wise men of Greece, who gave laws to Philocypros, King of [Soli]; though the Athenians claim him as theirs, because he appears in the lists of their Areopagites. Cleoboulos, a philosopher, son of Evagoras II, and Neocreon, who commanded the fleet of Alexander the Great, with others whom I omit. The church too found here several illustrious champions. St Barnabas, one of the 72 disciples, was born here, and here too suffered martyrdom. Mark, also called John, the cousin of St Barnabas. St Ariston, another of the 72 disciples, was martyred here. St Epiphanios, a bishop, of whom there are fuller notices in the *Illustrious men* of St Jerome, in Beda, and other ecclesiastical writers. By some St Catherine, daughter of King Costa, is said to be of Salamina, though all the collections of legends make her of Alexandria. There are authorities however who call her a Cypriot, among them a Greek legend, and a writer Pietro Calo. To the north of Salamina there still stands a small chamber in which they say she was confined, until she was removed to another prison in Paphos. When the Emperor Diocletian re-subdued Egypt, which had rebelled, he summoned to him from Cyprus King Costa. It was then that St Catherine was taken to Alexandria from her prison at Paphos, and there obtained the glorious palm of martyrdom. I leave such disputes to the ecclesiastical historians: they are no business of mine.

Along the shore between the ruins of Salamina and

Famagusta are many fields which produce *boià*, otherwise
madder-root (*robbia* or *lizari*). It furnishes a red dye, and is
one of the richest products of the island.

Following the coast eastward from Salamina you enter that
part of the island called Carpasso, which stretches up to Cape
St Andrea. I need only say that it produces abundantly silk
and cotton. On the seashore are groves of olive trees. They
are no longer fruitful, and are cut down for firewood. No one
hinders their destruction, and boats come even from the coast
towns of Syria to carry them away. The city anciently called
Carpassia is now the village of St John. The district is
governed by an *alai bey*, or captain of horse, who generally
lives at Varoshia, near Famagusta. There too resides a *Qazi*,
who acts as judge.

In the plain of Mesaria, about four miles from Salamina, is
a fine church dedicated to St Barnabas, and a large convent containing only a few Greek monks. A few years ago they wished
still further to enlarge the church, and had begun to lengthen
it by 25 *braccia*. But the permission was withdrawn, and the
monks forbidden to enlarge the church, lest some day it should
be used against the Grand Signor as a fortress. A liberal
bakhshish would have smoothed every difficulty.

A stone's throw hence stands another, older, church, almost
in ruins, dedicated to the same saint. Below this, in a
subterranean tomb, was laid the body of the saint, which was
discovered in the days of the Emperor Zenon. Many writers,
including the Roman martyrologists and Cardinal Baronius,
relate the story, and say that on the corpse was found the
Gospel of St Matthew, written by the evangelist's own hand.
The Greek bishop who presented the said Gospel to the
Emperor at Constantinople obtained the privilege of signing
his name with red ink, and in his full pontifical habit to wear
the crown, with the terrestrial globe in his left hand, and the
sceptre in his right, and the regal mantle—as well as of being
finally independent of the patriarch of Antioch, with whom

was a long pending dispute about precedence. The patriarch claimed that the bishopric of Cyprus was subject to the see of Antioch: the Cypriots would not allow this on the ground that theirs was the older church. The present archbishop of Cyprus enjoys all these privileges. I learned these details from various Cypriot monks, and their truth was confirmed by the archbishop Paisios.

CHAPTER XIV.

DEPARTURE FROM THE NEIGHBOURHOOD OF SALAMINA, AND RETURN TO LARNACA.

LEAVING the convent of St Barnabas, and crossing the plain of Mesaria towards the west, you reach a village called Angoni, where are large stores, used, when the plain was all under cultivation, to receive the harvest.

Still further west lies the large village of Trapezi. The ruins point to the site of a large city, and a Greek with whom I was travelling assured me that one had stood there: but the histories of the island in the sixteenth century call it a village, and make no mention of an earlier city. It has two churches, one of some size adorned with various marbles, with a porch supported by various marble columns. There are but few inhabitants, and the village seems a mere shelter for shepherds and the flocks they feed on the adjoining plain. [See S. Menardos, *Toponymicon*, p. 340.]

Turning south you reach on something of a hill Acerito, a village thickly inhabited and well cultivated. It is the property of Signor Andronico Caridis, (by *Berat*) honorary dragoman to H.I.M. the Apostolic Queen of Hungary. Near his residence is a little chapel dedicated to St Marina, of rough Greek construction, but embellished with fine old pictures of saints bought by him from houses in Famagusta at the price of the panels on which they are painted.

I stayed some days at Acerito during which I saw with

great regret the immense damage caused by the locusts, just at
the time that the grass is fresh, and grain in the ear. I will
quote in his own words, the account given by Benedetto
Bordone, in the third Book of his *Isolario*. After speaking of
the advantages enjoyed by the island, he goes on to describe
the destruction wrought by the locusts. " But among so many
blessings (so that there may be nothing in this world without
its bitterness) the luck and prosperity of the island are marred
by an evil of such gravity that for all its fertility it can hardly
bear up against it. This is the enormous quantity of *cavallette*
or locusts, which appear with the young crops, and in passing
from place to place so vast are their legions that like a thick
cloud they hide the sun. And where they light they devour
the corn, the grass, and the very roots below, so that you
would fancy a fire had blasted the ground. And this though
the inhabitants with all diligence give their time and money to
destroy them by digging out their eggs before the insects are
hatched. It may seem an exaggeration, but it is true that in
some years they find as many as 30,000 bushels. They try too
another most costly remedy, sending to Syria to fetch a certain
water, with which they drench the ground, and the eggs so
watered burst, and do not hatch out the insect." Things are
very different now. Then the peasants took all possible trouble
to extirpate the plague ; now they are forbidden to search for
the eggs, though at this stage the locusts are so easily
destroyed. It is the Turks who forbid them, because they
esteem it a capital sin to rebel against a Divine judgment, and
the Greeks let the creatures be, for fear of some fresh ill
treatment. Their chief habitat is the plain of Mesaria, and
when they appear one can only hope for a strong land breeze,
which carries out vast numbers to be drowned in the sea.
The remedies used from time to time to destroy the locusts
are described at the end of a Report, printed in 1717 at the
Grand Ducal press at Florence, of the operations in Tuscany,
where they appeared in great numbers in 1716.

On the road turning south from Acerito are several ancient churches, without a house near them. Each one had formerly its own village or hamlet; now some are partly ruined, some intact, and used occasionally by the Greeks for worship.

At the end of the plain of Mesaria, in a small valley, lies the village of Timbo, inhabited and tilled. It possesses a well of exquisite water, which makes it a favourite halting place for travellers from Famagusta and Carpasso.

From Timbo you descend a gentle hill to Fendria: the village is destroyed, the church, and country house built there by an English consul are in ruins. Following the seashore you leave on the right Livadia, a village described in my journey to Nicosia, and at twenty miles distance from Acerito reach Larnaca.

CHAPTER XV.

EXCURSION FROM LARNACA TO THE SALINES,
THE VILLAGE OF CITTI AND ITS NEIGHBOURHOOD.

Now that I have returned to the south of the island I will go on to describe the rest of its coast. Leaving Larnaca, and still keeping south, you pass the town of the Salines, and close to the church of St Lazarus, which I mentioned in my second chapter. It seems the proper place to speak of certain ancient Armenian inscriptions discovered in a wall of the enclosure of the church, which preserve the names and country of some devout Armenians, and the dates on which they came to express their reverence for the subterranean tomb which has been for many years considered the spot in which Lazarus, who was restored to life by our Lord, was buried the second time. As years passed the devotion to the place cooled down, perhaps because people grew convinced that the Lazarus was not he whom Christ raised from the dead, but a St Lazarus, bishop of Cyprus. If that be so or not I leave others to determine, here I will merely speak of the inscriptions, which have provoked some controversy among men of letters.

In 1766 the Chevalier Niebuhr, geometrician to the King of Denmark, visited Cyprus, and enquired about certain inscriptions, said to be somewhere about the church of St Lazarus, which Mr Swinton had supposed, with some hesitation, to be Phoenician. He went himself to the spot, and, for greater exactness, took with him a native called Parisin, a Maronite, who was conversant with various tongues, and acted as an interpreter to strangers. He had been, if I mistake not, also Mr Swinton's guide. Cav. Niebuhr was taken straight to these inscriptions, which had been already carefully examined by other foreigners. Cav. Niebuhr was an excellent Arabic scholar, and knew the characters of Chaldean, and other oriental languages. He saw at once that they could not be Phoenician. But, hesitating to rely upon his own judgment only, he made the best copies he could of the characters, which were strange to him and worn by time, and took these to Mr Timothy Turner, Her Britannic Majesty's consul in Cyprus, who thought them Armenian. I had seen the originals many times, and was always of the same opinion. Still we might be deceived, and we therefore sought out one Ambarsun, a native of Armenia, who read and wrote his own language well, to whom Cav. Niebuhr showed his copies, and asked him if he knew the character. He replied that he saw they were Armenian, but that it required some trouble to read them. However in our presence he made out the names, the country and the dates of some of the writers, and satisfied us that the inscriptions were really Armenian, engraved by some devout person who came to visit the church of St Lazarus. Other like records are found in every language in all the sanctuaries of Palestine.

I do not remember if Cav. Niebuhr carried away with him from Cyprus his copies of the inscriptions, but I fancy that when he knew them to be Armenian he set no further store on them, and left them as valueless. I grew equally indifferent, but to satisfy such men of letters as may wish to see them I will write to Cyprus, and do my best to obtain copies of them. Monsignor Mario Guarnacci, who has earned the gratitude of Italy by the many works in which he has illustrated its antiquities, speaks on p. 221 of the first volume of his *Origini Italiche* of Mr Swinton's opinion. He is inclined to think the characters are Pelasgian, or Etruscan, rather than Phoenician. I have laid before them the facts, and leave gentlemen of letters to exercise their wisdom thereon.

A mile from the church of St Lazarus is the great Salt Lake. Its old circumference was twelve miles; now a great part of it is dry and cultivated. The extent over which salt is now formed is little more than two miles, and it is about two hundred paces from the sea. The winter rains fill up this hollow, and in summer the heat of the sun congeals the surface to the depth of a palm, in some spots the salt covers the same depth of water. It is quite certain that the sea water does not get into it, and there used to be several ditches which carried the rain water to the sea, when this collected in such quantity that it might have hindered the formation of salt. These ditches are now out of repair, as well as the bridges which crossed them.

In August they break up the lake, and begin to extract the salt, taking care that it shall be all removed before the first rains, which would melt it. What they collect they pile in heaps like pyramids a few paces beyond the border of the lake. There it gets hard and resists all the winter rains, and in spring vessels begin to arrive from Syria to load it.

This product belongs to the Governor of the island, who lets the lake every year to the highest bidder. The lessee, as soon as his contract has expired, and he has not sold all his salt, cannot sell any after the commencement of the new lease. The surplus however remains his own, and he may leave it where it is until he obtains the lease again, but he generally agrees to sell it to the new lessee. In the days of the Venetians enough of this natural product was extracted every year to freight 70 vessels.

On the borders of the Salt Lake is a fine Turkish mosque called the Tekye. It is of octangular shape, and no expense has been spared to make the building solid: the foundations are good, and the stones large and squared. The Turks believe that here is the tomb of the mother of Mohammad, their false prophet. For many years it was but a small oratory, in charge of a Moslem monk, but it was not held in any great veneration until 1760. In the following year Ali Agha, Governor of Cyprus, erected the building mentioned above, which I saw completed, and the place began to grow in importance. Now it is so highly revered that no Turkish personage who visits the island fails to go to pray there, and even the ships that pass along this coast salute it with their guns. The mosque is under the care of a small college of Turkish Santons, who pass their lives in their usual extravagant austerities.

In the neighbourhood is an enclosure with many orange, lemon and other fruit trees, and flowers. There is no order or arrangement, but the place has a certain charm, and is a favourite resort of the people of Larnaca. The garden was planted by some Pasha, a former governor of Cyprus, and is still called the Pasha's garden.

Returning to the road which leads from the Salines to Citti, you reach the village of Meneou. The lands are under cultivation, but there are few inhabitants. It used to be a very large village, but is now ruined, and a Greek church which had survived until 1760 was then destroyed, and the stones used in the building of the Tekye. A little to the right you see the village of Arpera, where are the springs which feed the aqueducts by which Larnaca is supplied with water, and at last you come to Citti, four miles from the Salines.

Citti is the village mentioned in my third chapter, where I showed that Lusignan was wrong in calling it the ancient city of Citium, for it was never anything but a village, which took its name from the promontory of the ancient Citium half a mile away. It was once a *fief* of one of the houses of Lusignan, and even now shows some signs of its old importance. The church is large, and dedicated to the Virgin, whose picture in mosaic is venerated by the Greeks. In the middle of the village is a large and deep well of excellent water, the work of Chiarione de Lusignan. One can go down to the bottom of it. Opposite it stood an old fortress; on a part of its foundations the Turks have built a square tower, to which the inhabitants, the women especially, retire, when they fear the descent of Christian corsairs on the coast. Beyond the village is a stone bridge of several arches, with sluices, no longer in repair, which during the rains allowed the water to flood the fields, and turned it again into the river, when they had been watered enough. Much cotton was grown here; now the land is more used for wheat, barley, and mulberry trees. The yield of silk is abundant. Near the sea are a few country houses, belonging to merchants in Larnaca. It may not be the pleasantest of resorts, but at least it is the nearest to their homes in the town.

CHAPTER XVI.

JOURNEY FROM THE VILLAGE OF CITTI
TO THE CITY OF LIMASOL.

KEEPING along the coast west of Citti, at no great distance from the sea, you see the village of Mazoto, which takes its name from the cape close by. I need not describe this, nor other places along the road, which leads to the torrent Vasilo-potamos, 25 miles from Citti. Vasilopotamos is a Greek word, meaning the Royal River: they say the stream was so named when Helene, mother of Constantine the Great, landed there on her return from Jerusalem. Its ancient name, as we find it in old maps, was Tezio. It was one of the four large streams in the island, and hence perhaps the name Vasilopotamos.

About three miles from the sea, on this very river, was a city called Marium, which gave its name to the village Marin, which rose out of its ruins. Marin still keeps its name, though it is oftener called Vasilopotamos or St George, from a church and convent of Greek monks a little way off. There are many carob trees about it, and in summer vessels come here to load the fruit, but in summer only, because captains find the place at other seasons too open to the winds, and too dangerous for their ships.

Twelve miles from Vasilopotamos is old Limasol, so called by the Greeks to distinguish it from the other Limasol, of which I shall speak presently. It is a mere ruin of a town, with a few remains to show that it was once an important city. It was so, and remained such under the Dukes who governed Cyprus for the Greek Emperors of Constantinople. Isaac the last of these was conquered by Richard, King of England, who destroyed the city in 1191. It was never rebuilt. Here stood ancient Amathus, in which was a temple dedicated to Venus and Adonis, see Pausanias, lib. IX.: "Amathus is a city in Cyprus, in it there is an ancient temple of Adonis and Aphrodite." Amathus was the seat of one of the nine Kings, and [Rhoicos reigned there, cir. B.C. 351].

Under the Christians it was a bishopric, and produced men famous for their piety and learning, among whom was the bishop Leontius, who flourished about A.D. 590, and was still alive in A.D. 616; he wrote the life of St John the Almoner, Patriarch of Alexandria, also a native of Amathus; St Tychon, consecrated bishop by St Epiphanios, in the reign of Arcadius; and in the Greek Menologies are commemorated other saints who came from this city, as St Stadion and St Mnemonios. All about the place are copper mines, which have been abandoned since the Turks took the island. These were famous in Ovid's day, *Met.* x. 220,

> Won by his manly beauty, Cythera no longer allures her:
> Cnidos, the haunt of fishers, and Paphos too are forsaken,
> Paphos' sea-girt walls, and Amathus' earthborn treasure.

The spot on which the present city of Limasol stands was formerly called Nemosia, from its many groves. After Richard, King of England, had destroyed Amathus, Guy de Lusignan in the twelfth century began to build the new city, which the Greeks called Neapolis; and as time went on, it was enlarged by other Lusignans, fortified and adorned with palaces, Latin and Greek churches, and was made a bishopric. When the Turks came in 1570 to take the island on July 2 they sacked and burned the city: it is but a poor place now, with a few

remains of ancient buildings. It is governed by a Commissioner: there is a *Qazi* also, but cases must be referred for
decision to the Governor at Nicosia.

The roadstead is convenient, being sheltered from the
fiercer winds: so that vessels take refuge here from the bad
weather outside. Carobs are largely exported, for the best
crops are gathered here. Salt too is collected from a salt lake
not far off, which is not so large as that near Citti. A custom-
house, with a chief or *Agha*, regulates the trade. Cotton,
wheat, barley and mulberry trees are cultivated with care and
yield abundantly. And other food stuffs are produced.
Among the hills and mountains which stand at some distance
from Limasol is made the best wine in Cyprus. It all comes
down in due season to the town, and is sent thence to Larnaca,
where are the largest cellars, and the most considerable wine
trade.

CHAPTER XVII.

JOURNEY FROM LIMASOL TO PAPHOS.

BEYOND Limasol was Curi, an ancient city on Cape delle Gatte. It is entirely destroyed, the only existing remains being a few marble columns. There is a church dedicated to St Nicolas, and a convent of Greek monks called, like the village, Acrotiri. A mile and a half from Acrotiri, and about three miles from the sea, is a village called Colosso, with a strong castle, built by the Knights Templars, held first by them, and then by the Hospitallers, or Knights of Malta.

Before reaching Piscopia you cross a torrent, known to ancient geographers as one of the chief rivers of Cyprus, under the name Lycus. The village of Piscopia is six miles from Cape delle Gatte : it lies in a plain which produces the best cotton in the island. In the time of the Venetians it was planted with sugar canes, but these were abandoned when the cultivation of cotton proved more profitable. The village is still one of the most flourishing in Cyprus, it has abundant water, a pleasant situation, and lemon, orange, olive and other fruit-bearing trees in plenty. It gave a name to the noble Venetian house of Cornara Piscopia.

The fine remains found under the village confirm the opinion of those authors who place here Curium, the capital city of one of the nine Kings. [Herodotus, v. 113, gives the name of a King Stasanor, who deserted to the Persians in B.C. 498.]

Nine miles from Curium is Afdimu, a village of few inhabitants but not badly cultivated. It was one of [the four cities in the island built by Ptolemy Philadelphus in honour of his sister Arsinoe.

Twelve miles further on is Conuclia, the residence of an *Agha*, the principal person in these parts, and looked on as a kind of feudal lord. The land round the village, owing to the abundance of running water, produces silk and excellent cotton. Many curious antiquities used to be found here, especially in tombs. Now the Turks view all excavations with jealousy, and everyone fears in attempting such to expose himself to fresh extortions. Here stood the city Cythera so besung by poets. It was sacred to Venus, and gave of old a name to the island, as Pliny, Strabo and others tell us.

The next site on the south coast is Old Paphos. Here was the famous temple of Venus, overthrown, together with the entire city, by an earthquake. Scarcely any remains are visible. A lake close by is not always dry in summer, and makes the place somewhat unhealthy.

Nea-Paphos or New Paphos is on the east coast. It was so called by ancient geographers, and is still known as Pafo, though the name in some modern maps is written Baffo. But it is no longer a city such as historians describe it, having been more than once destroyed. It had a harbour, and even now vessels coming to load here anchor outside; but only in summer, for it is the most dangerous roadstead in the island, exposed and with a bad and rocky bottom, which does great damage to the cables, which are sometimes cut through. Sailors take care to buoy them off the bottom with empty casks, which keep them suspended in the water. There is a fort on the shore, and another, ruined, on the adjacent hill.

Pafo is governed by a *Digdaban* or Commissioner; there is also a *Qazi* and an *Agha*, who is Customs officer. The only building of Christian times is the church of St George, now used by Greeks. The products of this end of the island are cotton, silk, wheat and barley, all abundant and of excellent quality.

He would fish in troubled waters who would try to trace the origin of either city, Old or New Paphos, and I leave the question as too difficult for me. I may just say that in New Paphos too was a temple of Venus, which was destroyed, together with the city, by an earthquake. St Paul, on his visit to Paphos (Acts xiii.) converted by his preaching the Roman Proconsul Sergius Paulus. Here too he adopted as his disciple and follower Titus, whom he ordained deacon in the city in which he afterwards suffered martyrdom. Pafo was the seat of a bishop under the Lusignans, and has still a Greek bishop, a suffragan of the archbishop of Nicosia.

CHAPTER XVIII.

JOURNEY FROM PAFO TO LAPITO.

THERE are a good many villages scattered here and there about the eastern end of the island, none of them are of any consequence, and some are abandoned and in ruins, so I will not attempt to enumerate them. Those that I shall describe, though their present prosperity may be small, at least made some figure in the works of ancient writers.

Beyond Pafo lies Cape St Epifanio, anciently called Cape Acama, and near it a large village. More to the north is the Gulf of Crusocco, so called from the village Crusocco, the ancient Acamantis, one of the nine royal cities. In the neighbourhood were veins and mines of gold, and here too they made vitriol. The lands about this bay produce the best wheat in the island. Near it is the so-called Fontana Amorosa [Ariosto, *Orl. Fur.* xviii. 136] and the city of Calinusa, known also as Alexandretta, now a hamlet.

Next comes the Gulf of Pentaia, and a large village called Lefca, rich in cotton plants and mulberry trees. The abundance of water here encouraged the cultivation of the sugar cane, which is now abandoned throughout the island. One of the four cities called Arsinoe stood on this site.

Solia, in a pretty situation, 24 miles from Pafo, is a large village, producing excellent cotton, silk, barley and wheat. St Eusebius, who was baptised by St Mark the Evangelist, was bishop of Solia, as were also the martyrs St Ammonius and St Alexander. Under the Lusignans the Greek bishop who resided in Nicosia bore the title of bishop of Solia. Monsignore Galletti di Arezzo, now bishop-coadjutor of Volterra, is bishop of Solia, *in partibus.* Here stood the city Aipeia, which took its later name of Soloi from Solon, who rebuilt it at the instance of Philocypros, King of [Soli], as Plutarch in his life of Solon relates at length. This was the last of the royal cities, as they existed about B.C. 600. Eighteen miles from Solia is the village Cormachiti, called after the cape on which it is built. It was once a city named Cormia.

Next follows Lapito, one of the largest villages in Cyprus. It is pleasantly situated, and abounds in all the most valued products of the island. Fruit is generally scarce, but here at least it is fairly plentiful. It was the ancient city Lapethos, whose foundation is ascribed to the Spartans, and a capital of one of the nine Kings, of whom [Praxippos, deposed by Ptolemy, B.C. 312], was the last. Venus had a temple here. A river or torrent of the same name runs by the village: its stream never fails, and contributes greatly to the fertility of the country. Six miles east of Lapito is the castle of Cerines, described in Chap. VIII.

CHAPTER XIX.

OF SOME VILLAGES AND HAMLETS AND OTHER INLAND PLACES IN CYPRUS.

TREMITUGIA is a village 12 miles to the west of Nicosia. It was formerly a city called Tremitus, destroyed by Richard, King of England, when he took the island. Ptolemaeus, the geographer, put it in his list of the cities of Cyprus (lib. v. 4, Asia, c. XIV.) St Spyridon, a native of Cyprus, was bishop of Tremitus, and was present in A.D. 325 at the Council of Nicaea. There are full accounts of him in the *Ecclesiastical History* of Socrates, I. 12, and that of Sozomen, I. 11. Its lands, like those of the inland villages generally, are devoted to all kinds of food stuffs, with cotton, silk, olives and wine.

Dali is a village on a hill, 12 miles south of Nicosia. The situation is pleasant, and even beautiful, for there are little woods round it, excellent water, and a quantity of sweet smelling herbs, particularly marjoram. Virgil mentions it, *Aeneid* I. 691 (Bowen)

"Over the limbs of her Ascan the tranquil waters of sleep
Venus bestows, then bears him to groves on Idalia's steep,
Lulled on her bosom. Beneath him a yielding amaracus laid
Folds him in bright hued flowers and in fragrant bowery shade."

The ancient city was called Idalium, one of the four Cypriot cities dedicated to Venus. So Virgil again, *Aeneid* X. 51,

"Amathus too is mine, and the towering fanes of Paphos,
Mine are Idalium's groves, and the flowering shades of Cythera."

The ancient name of the village Tamagia, which is in the direction of Famagusta, was Tamasus, and it is so called by the geographer Ptolemaeus, v. 14. Pliny however calls it Tamasos, v. 130, and Ovid, *Met.* x. 644 says: "there is a tract, the natives call it Tamasenus, the richest part of the land of Cyprus." Gold, copper and vitriol were formerly found here.

Arcios, once a city, is now an inland village in the district of Paphos.

Pellandros, once a city called Palea, is now a large village, which makes much wine, 24 miles from Limasol towards Mt Olympus. Other wine-producing villages are Zopi, Omodos, Limnari, once a city, and Eftagonia, which has also a vein of gold.

At Cicco, a village situated on a spur of Mt Olympus, 60 miles from Nicosia, the Greeks have a monastery, with 150 monks of the order of St Basil, in which is a renowned picture of the Virgin Mary. The name of the convent is Trigugiotissa, but the people usually call it Cicco. The Cypriots greatly venerate this picture, and resort in crowds to a feast and fair held in its honour on the eighth of September, old style.

Mt Olympus, called by the Greeks Throdos, is in extension and height the first mountain in the island. On its slopes are several convents of Greek monks, fewer however now than of old. In one part of it the snow is preserved all through the summer. A little village near is freed by the Turkish Government from all burdens except that of carrying this snow to the palace of the Governor at Nicosia throughout the summer.

On Cape Cormachiti, a little inland, lies the large village of Gambeli; an *Agha*, with limited powers, lives there. Its cotton is excellent.

At Calopsidia with the ashes of the herb soda they make soap of indifferent quality. Among many other villages I may mention Ipso, Latrico, Morfu, Corno and Bergamo. Each of them has a church of the Greek rite.

Lefcara is a fine village at the foot of Mt Olympus, with a church dedicated to the Holy Cross. It has abundant water, and produces good cotton crops. Here too they collect ladanum.

Chibaiani, 18 miles from Limasol in the direction of Mt Olympus, produces much wine. Here was a city called Corineum or Curreo, near which Richard, King of England, routed Duke Isaac.

Amiantus, near Pellandros, was a large place in the days of the Romans. They dug hence the stone amiantus, from which they made the bags in which they burnt the corpses of their Emperors.

The castle of the god of Love, 15 miles to the north of Nicosia, was destroyed by the Venetians, who did not wish to have a number of small fortresses scattered about the island. It is now called after St Hilarion, who died here A.D. 371 at the age of 80, and was buried in a garden, where now stands a church erected in his honour, for he is greatly venerated by the Greeks. After resting here one year his body was carried to Egypt, as says St Jerome in his life of the saint (vol. II. col. 39, 40, ed. Migne, Paris, 1845).

In Pirga and Anglipsidia are many olive trees, planted symmetrically at equal distances so that they form a kind of grove. Some of them are so thick that two men can hardly join their arms round them. I am sure they must be extremely old, and they are generally admired as the finest trees of their kind.

Mt Santa Croce, 18 miles from Larnaca, is considered a spur of Mt Olympus, though it stands quite distinct from it. Being at no great distance from the southern shore, it is a landmark to direct mariners to the roadstead of Larnaca. If they drop their anchor as soon as they have the mountain full in face they are quite sure of finding safe moorings. Ships which come in by day never fail to see it, for however thick the clouds lie over the plain and about its slopes the top itself

is never hidden.   Olympus on the other hand, and the hills
round it are lost to sight in the slightest mist.

On the summit is a church dedicated to the Holy Cross,
built by St Helena after her return from Jerusalem.   A convent
of Greek monks adjoining it is partly destroyed, but still gives
an idea of its former size and solidity.   In the church is
preserved a fragment of our Saviour's Cross, as long as half a
finger, and as thick as one's thumb.   In later years doubt has
been thrown on this relic, and this is the reason.   Some Greek
priests of the village of Lefcara, mentioned above, conceived
the idea of robbing the convent of so remarkable a relic to
glorify their own church by its presence, and framed a cunning
tale that a similar piece of the True Cross had been lately
presented to them, which they wished to compare with that on
the mountain, whose authenticity they knew to be indisputable,
as it had come from the hands of St Helena herself.   These
wily Lefcariots received permission to do so, and went over to
the mountain with a sham relic so fashioned as exactly to
resemble the true.   When the two pieces were brought together
they began to shuffle them about, and to wrangle over them,
until at last no one knew which was the piece of the True Cross,
each party claiming that honour for their own.   The people
continue to have more faith in that on the mountain, but
frequent also the feast held at Lefcara; for opinions are divided,
and to this day disputes and quarrels agitate the priests of the
two churches.

Traces of gold and copper are found on the mountain.
At the foot of its steepest side is a church dedicated to St
Barbara, served by a few of the monks from the convent on
the top.   Commanderia is a tract lying between Limasol, Pafo
and Mt Olympus.   It takes its name from the great Commandery of St John, and that of the Knights Templars, which
embraced all these villages.   The most exquisite wine and the
best muscat grapes are produced here, and called hence wines
of the Commandery, as though to mark their superiority over

all the other wines of the island.   There are many ruins of
buildings and small forts, but none of them older than the
days of the Lusignan Kings.

I have now completed my description of the cities, villages
and hamlets of Cyprus as well those which lie inland as those
on the sea coast.   I hope my readers will not be sorry to have
five further chapters.   In the first I shall tell the story of a
rebellion which occurred in Cyprus only a few years ago.   In
the second I shall treat of the commerce, in the third of the
consuls, in the fourth of the consular officers, and in the fifth
of the subjects of European sovereigns, and of other persons
who enjoy consular protection.

CHAPTER XX.

OF AN INSURRECTION WHICH OCCURRED A SHORT WHILE SINCE IN THE ISLAND OF CYPRUS.

CYPRUS had suffered for many years from the incessant, heavy and unjust burdens imposed on its inhabitants by the caprice of successive Governors, in spite of the commands issued by the Sultan to prevent such exactions. In 1764 Chil Osman Agha, Governor of the island, outdid all his predecessors, for he had scarcely taken over the government in July of this year than he published a decree, ordering the collection from every Christian subject of the Sultan 44½ piastres Turkish, and from every Turk half that sum, being double the *Kharaj* or annual poll tax assigned to the Governors of the island by the Sultan. In just five months, according to an accurate reckoning, besides the said tax he had probably encashed 350,000 piastres extorted from persons falsely accused of crimes.

The bishops on behalf of the Christians, and the leading Turks for the Muslims, did not fail to submit their grievances to the Governor, and to pray him to abate his demands, showing him that it was impossible that all alike could satisfy them. Their kindly efforts elicited no other answer than that the order must be carried out: if they thought the tax exorbitant, let them appeal to the Grand Signor for redress of the injustice which they ascribed to him.

When the bishops and leading Turks saw that the Governor was inflexible, they thought it well to inform the Porte of the injustice daily practised, and deputed certain persons to go to Constantinople to obtain a rescript in their favour. The bishops, fearing that the common cause was not being pushed at Constantinople with zeal worthy of the emergency, determined to go there in person; but their plan was discovered, and they were detained and put under arrest. They were thus obliged to wait the return of their agents, who arrived on October 31, accompanied by a *Vezir Choqadar*, an official of the Grand Vezir's Court, bearing three orders. The first commanded the Governor not to exact from each Christian, as *Kharaj*, more than 20 piastres, and 10 from a Turk, and to restore all that he had collected beyond that amount. A second ordered a rigorous investigation concerning all sums exacted upon lying charges, and restitution to be made thereof. A third was addressed to the persons who had counselled the Governor to such acts of extortion.

On the morning of November 5 the *Vezir Choqadar* proceeded to the *Mehkeme* or *Qazi's* Court, and sent thence a summons to the Governor to attend the Court and hear the purport of these decrees. He excused himself, and begged the *Vezir Choqadar* to be so good as to come to the palace, and read the decrees there. The *Vezir Choqadar* made no difficulty, and bade the bishops and leading men in Nicosia, both Turks and Greeks, to attend the reading at the palace.

A large crowd assembled in the courtyard to hear the conclusion of so vital a matter, and many others were in the *divan*, or hall of audience, but the first order had scarcely been read when the part of the room in which stood the bishops and other principal Turks and Christians, fell in, and carried down with it some 300 persons. The catastrophe caused great confusion, and many people suspected it to be a trick pre-arranged by the Governor, whereon the *Molla* or chief judge, the *Choqadar* and others went to examine the place, and found that the Governor had caused the beams and pillars which supported the floor to be sawn through, so that when pulled with ropes the whole fell in.

The malicious cruelty of the Governor did not end here, for, foreseeing that the *Choqadar*, who sat next to himself, would not be hurled down with the rest, he caused poisoned coffee to be served to him. Luckily the collapse of the room did not produce the desired effect; only four or five persons were slightly injured, and the *Choqadar*, promptly treated with antidotes, suffered no harm.

The crowd saw what had happened, and rushed at once to the *Molla* to ask for justice. Three several summonses were sent to the Governor, who refused to appear, using some sharp expressions. The *Molla* could no longer restrain the people, who kept thronging in with cries for justice, and decided to allow them to do what they liked with the Governor, proclaiming him a rebel to the law and to his sovereign.

These words at once excited the crowd to rush in arms to the palace. The Governor did not lose courage, but barred the gates, and retired with all his train to the upper rooms, whence he fired on the assailants, and killed several. Some of the crowd began to fire back, while others were setting fire to the gates of the great court. As soon as these were burnt down men rushed in, killed everyone they met and at last had the satisfaction of finding the Governor himself, whom they despatched with knife thrusts. Nineteen persons of his suite were killed, the rest escaped and hid themselves until the fury was overpast. As soon as the Governor was dead everyone betook himself to plunder the *Khasna* or Treasury, and to strip the palace of its furniture. The whole affair took three hours: the tact of the Turkish headmen quelled the disturbance, and before evening the shops were all reopened, the fair of St Demetrius went on, and the city resumed its usual aspect, as though nothing had happened.

The citizens of Larnaca were expecting the same tragic

fate for their *Digdaban*, a faithful imitator of his chief's injustice; but the *Qazi* managed cleverly to get him into his
house, and quieted the people by promises that he should be
punished according to law. His judicious conduct prevented
any attack which might have been projected on the houses of
the rich Turks, Greeks and Europeans. On November 10 the
Choqadar left for Constantinople to report to the Grand Vezir
what had happened.

After the murder of Chil Osman the island went on peace-
fully; there was no one to exercise absolute power, but there
was no motive to worry the people with heavy taxes, and
everyone looked after his own affairs. At last a new *Muhassil*,
or Governor, arrived from Constantinople, Hafiz Mohammad
Efendi, a man of capacity and tact. The people were satisfied,
seeing that for the present no search was made for the recusants, or for those who had taken part in the attack on his
predecessor. During Ramadhan, the annual Moslem fast, he
went down to Larnaca to make himself known there.

On his return to Nicosia he pursued the same conciliatory
policy, but his courtiers, to curry favour with him, began to
furnish the names of some of those who helped to excite the
insurrection of November 5, 1764. He found himself at last
obliged, as it were, to abandon his attitude of indifference,
particularly when he came to know the very men who had
taken a personal share in the murder of Chil Osman Agha.
Still, when he considered the danger of meting out condign
punishment, he consulted his own interests only, and issued
a proclamation to the effect that he had been appointed
Governor to restore order in the island, and to behead all
those who were accused of complicity in the recent riot: that
this time however he would be satisfied if the people at large,
Greeks and Turks alike, would purchase forgiveness by the
payment of 14 piastres a head, women, minors and cripples
alone being exempted.

People began to pay the tax, until some Turk persuaded

many of his friends to refuse. They gave as their reason that they claimed to be recognised by the Sultan as men who had freed the Empire from a tyrant, who was bent on destroying rather than preserving the provinces. Were they to be subjected to a fixed fine they would be admittedly rebels, a stigma they could in no wise bear, for they boasted themselves to be liberators of their country, and protectors of justice. However they soon saw that these excuses would not exempt them from the payment of the 14 piastres, and some hundreds of them openly mutinied, and assembled in force in the village of Citerea, where are the flour mills which supply Nicosia, cut off the water and turned it into fresh channels, so as to prevent the mills from working, and the city from receiving its daily supply. Nicosia was in an uproar, and the Governor, seeing the people ready for a rising of a graver kind, settled the matter as best he could, and persuaded the malcontents to withdraw from Citerea by promises that no further demand should be made for the 14 piastres.

Meanwhile the archbishop and the bishops of Pafo and Cerines, the bishop of Citium only being left behind, had gone secretly to Constantinople to represent the exactions to which the island was subjected at the hands of each new *Muhassil*. A new Governor was promised them, who arrived a few months later. During their absence the Governor Hafiz, seeing the people quiet again, began to demand afresh the 14 piastres. A few paid it, but the collection was very slow, and on August 12, 1765, Hafiz heard of a new band of recusants, whose chief, greatly to the Governor's alarm, proved to be one Khalil Agha, Commandant of the castle of Cerines, in whose charge were all the arms and warlike stores. They based this renewed movement solely on their determination not to pay the poll tax. Their cause became that of the whole people, and volunteers arrived every day to swell the band of Khalil Agha.

The Governor immediately closed the gates of the capital.

The rising was as popular as it was sudden, the mutineers were already 2000 in number, and had again seized the mills at Citerea, which they worked for their own needs only, while some of them were posted under the walls of Nicosia to prevent supplies entering the city.

On August 18 the citizens made a sortie, but were promptly driven back by the rebels. These however saw that to hold out much longer they must strengthen their numbers, and began to impress the Turks, burning the houses and even the villages of the recusants, and so increased their force to 3000. On August 28 the Governor saw that the rebellion was spreading over the island, and bethinking himself of the straits in which he would find himself when the capital began to lack food, came to terms with the malcontents and promised and swore that he would never again exact money as the price of pardon, and that he had freely forgiven everybody. A calm followed, the gates were opened, and people went about their business. The mutineers however kept ready to assemble in case of need.

Presently a French ship arrived with the bishops, and the servants and baggage of the new Governor, Suleiman Efendi, who landed shortly after at Cerines. By favours and presents he won over to the side of order Khalil Agha, head of the rebels, and praised openly his zeal for the common prosperity. This diplomatic flattery opened to him a safe passage from Cerines to Nicosia, but he entirely failed in inducing Khalil Agha to follow him, although his liberal offers included even the post of *alai bey*, or general of the cavalry. Khalil Agha knew how little he could trust this sudden politeness.

On the arrival of Suleiman Efendi at Nicosia the island had two Governors, but Hafiz Mohammad Efendi refused absolutely to abandon his post until the rebellion was finally crushed, for up to this point he had gallantly defended the city. Suleiman made no objection, for he was an aged man, chiefly interested in his own comfort.

So matters stood up to the beginning of the new year 1766, when some new impulse united the two *Muhassils*, and it was decided for the third time to insist on the collection of the 14 piastres. The recusants immediately left their houses again, and mustered, to the number of 5000 persons, under the standard of Khalil Agha. On January 10 their chief sent a party of 500 to Famagusta, knowing of how great value its capture would be; but though its armed defenders numbered scarcely 100 it proved impregnable. On the 24th he abandoned the attack on Famagusta, and with the whole rebel band took up his position before Nicosia. The gates were again closed, and cannon mounted on the walls. Khalil Agha refused to break up his camp, and a messenger was sent out of the city to inquire his terms. He demanded to be Governor of the island, and to enter Nicosia. To this silly request no answer was given. Presently he sent word to the Governor that this was no freak of his own, but an order from the sovereign, which he invited the Governor and his council to come out to the camp to hear—a trick which did not deceive the wily *Muhassil*. The rebels meanwhile made several attempts to scale the walls; but these were badly planned and wholly failed, involving the lives of some of the assailants. Several sallies and skirmishes of little moment followed, while the defenders of Nicosia, some 1500 only, were obliged to look after the safety of their houses.

January 27 was a day of great anxiety to the inhabitants of Larnaca, particularly the Europeans, who imagined that the rebels might swoop down on the town, and strip their houses. Confusion reigned, and everyone was busy packing up his most valuable effects, and sending them with the women on board the ships of Christian Powers which happened to be in the roadstead. The next morning the alarm was seen to be false, their fears vanished, and all was quiet again.

At the beginning of February the island generally was

disturbed, and trade suspended.   The farms were left untilled, many houses were abandoned, and the insurgents began to force even old servants of the government to join their band. They appeared openly in Larnaca, and asked for arms, powder and warlike stores, applying personally to Europeans, and even at the consular houses.   On the other hand the government at Nicosia kept threatening all who helped Khalil Agha and his followers.

The leading Turks in Larnaca, merchants and others, together with the *Digdaban* or Commissioner, the Customs officer and *Sirdar* conceived the notion of arranging through the consuls of the Christian princes a truce between the government and the rebels, upon terms which would satisfy both.   They approached the French consul, who excused himself on the ground that the King, his master, forbade him to interfere in matters affecting the local government which had no relation with his own duties.   They passed on to Mr Timothy Turner, British consul and Tuscan vice-consul, who was always ready to help everyone, but he declined this mission unless he had the concurrence and help of the consuls of France and Venice.   They refused to interfere, and again Mr Turner was entreated to take upon himself alone the negotiation.   He firmly declined, and bowed the Turkish magnates out of his room, saying that except in concert with his colleagues he could not possibly intervene.

The Turks, who knew of how much weight Mr Turner's mediation would be, came back to him and warned him that he would be the cause of greater misfortunes which might yet befal the island, and that the people would always reproach him as the author of their disasters.

The consul, thus hard pressed, tried to see how tranquillity might be restored, at least until some efficient succour arrived from without.   From the general talk of the malcontents he gathered that their demands would be comprised in the four following articles:

1. A general amnesty.

2. A declaration under the Governor's seal that he would levy no taxes from the people beyond what were expressly commanded by the Grand Signor.

3. That the *Za'im*, a kind of commissioners, and the Janissaries who had taken part in the revolt should be restored to their posts and pay.

4. That the inhabitants of Nicosia should give a declaration under their seal that they wished Khalil Agha to be Governor, if he were approved by the Sultan.

Mr Turner satisfied himself that these were the main points of the rebels' demands, and communicated them to the Commissioner of Larnaca, asking him if they would be accepted by his chief at Nicosia. The *Digdaban* assured him that the *Muhassil* would have no difficulty in admitting them all: the first two were quite in accordance with his own desire to please the people, the two last would be dealt with as it might please the Sultan to approve or reject them.

After Mr Turner had received the assurance of this officer, who ought to know something of his chief's ideas, he wrote to Khalil Agha that he had accepted the office of mediator to restore peace to the island. The *Digdaban* wrote in the same sense to the Governor. Khalil Agha returned a polite answer to Mr Turner, assuring him of his readiness to open negotiations; but the messenger sent by the *Digdaban* to the Governor fell on his return into the hands of a skirmishing party of the rebels, who robbed him of his despatches. This incident determined Mr Turner not to proceed further until he knew the real feelings of the *Muhassil*; but all the Turks of Larnaca thought it expedient that he should go to the camp of Khalil Agha, address thence a letter to the Governor, and await his answer, and this he decided to do. The consul then arranged his affairs at Larnaca as best he could, and leaving me in charge set out on February 13, 1766, with MM. Stefano Saraf, a Tuscan merchant, and Pietro Crutta, dragoman. The

Commissioner of Larnaca, the *Qazi*, the *Sirdar* and other Turkish notables joined them, and the next day they arrived at the camp where Khalil Agha received them all with every possible civility.

He wrote immediately to the Governor, and on the 15th received his reply, inviting him to the city. He went there the same day with the four articles. The Governor's reply was given in general terms, that as the Sultan had confided to him the charge of the whole island and particularly of the fortress of Nicosia, the seat of the Government, he could not depart from his instructions without the express order of his sovereign, but if the rebels would retire, each to his own home, he offered them a general amnesty.

On the 16th the consul brought out this answer to the insurgents, who held inflexible to the last two points of their demand. He abandoned the negotiations, and returned to the city, to take leave of the *Muhassil* and go down to Larnaca. But when he was on the point of starting the people resolutely opposed his departure, saying that since his arrival in Nicosia they were no longer annoyed by the insurgents, and this interval of quiet was due to the respect paid by Khalil Agha's followers to his person and character. This was on February 17, on which day the consul finding himself in this singular situation contrived that a letter should reach me, in which he conveyed a succinct account of what had happened, formally appointed me his deputy at Larnaca, and showed me how I might maintain with him a correspondence intelligible to ourselves only.

I was pleased to think that Mr Turner could thus contribute towards the general peace of the island, but my pleasure was short-lived, for I saw every day my house full of rebels who demanded arms and ammunition, and knew on the other hand that I was watched to see if I favoured the insurgents to the detriment of the Government. I was anxious for his return, when on the 22nd, I heard that some Turkish men of war, fully armed, had arrived at Limasol to assist the island.   I informed the consul, so that he might take the news to the Governor, and then persuade the people, who might now expect armed help, to let him return.   The inhabitants waited for the news to be confirmed, and then let him go. He arrived on February 25th—Signor Saraf had managed to leave Nicosia on the 23rd—and I was glad enough to resign my duties at Larnaca.   As soon as Mr Turner left, hostilities were renewed, and the rebels again attacked the capital.

Meanwhile the vessels whose arrival had been announced at Limasol came on to Larnaca; they were two small galliots commanded by Ibrahim Bey with 150 men, a force too small to be effective.   They attempted negotiations, and when these failed put out again to sea.   The rebels meanwhile kept their position before Nicosia, brought up several cannon, and began to use them against the city.

On June 6 Ja'far Bey, captain of a Turkish privateer, arrived in the roadstead of the Salines with one war vessel, one xebec, and two half galleys.   With the intention of restoring peace to the island he landed 200 men, and took possession of the fort in the town.   His soldiers were guilty of every kind of excess, and very soon were hated more than the rebels, who had never done the least harm to private persons. The next day Khalil Agha sent to Larnaca a detachment of 500 of his followers to ask Ja'far Bey why he had landed and seized the fort, and to express his wonder that he had dared to take such a step, for the fort and the whole island were well guarded for the Sultan by faithful subjects, lovers of justice.   If they had need to defend themselves against a foreign foe they did not want the help of a pirate and his handful of insolent rascals.

Ja'far Bey was somewhat embarrassed by this attack, but took no stronger measures than to draw up his few men under arms.   Several proposals were made, the last being to wait the decision of Khalil Agha, to whom a message was sent.   A truce was concluded, and the soldiers on both sides retired to their quarters. On the 9th Ja'far Bey learnt that matters were taking an unfavourable turn: towards evening he gave up the fort, re-embarked his soldiers, and with them some Turkish notables and the Customs officer; and sailed the same night for Famagusta. There he landed his passengers and some of his soldiers, and put out again to sea.

On the 11th a detachment of the insurgents returned to Larnaca, marched to the town of Salines, and took possession of the fort, upon which they hoisted the Sultan's standard, proclaiming themselves the defenders of their sovereign's strongholds.

On the 27th a certain Qarqa Oghlu, Governor of Selefka, a town in Caramania, arrived at Famagusta with some transports and 200 soldiers. On the same day Kior Mohammad, a Pasha of two tails, arrived in the roadstead of Salines from Satalia on a Turkish war vessel, commanded by Meleky Bey, and accompanied by several transports of different nations carrying 2000 troops and 500 horses. These expeditions were sent by the Porte to put down the rebels, and restore order. The consular dragomans went on board to welcome the Pasha, who received them with great courtesy, but asked only general questions about the state of the island.

The soldiers of Qarqa Oghlu landed and made forays in the neighbourhood of Famagusta, allowing themselves every license, and robbing houses and dishonouring their inmates. The very men from whom the island should have obtained relief were the authors of worse outrages than even the rebels had committed. Their barbarity was carried so far that they seized seven Greeks, and impaled them outside the gate of the city, and beheaded two Turks, without themselves knowing why, unless it were to gratify the natural savagery of Caramanians, and of their chief Qarqa Oghlu.

On the 29th the rebels, who had occupied the fort in the

town of Salines, evacuated it, and retired to their fortified lines before Nicosia.   On the 30th Kior Mohammad Pasha landed, and went to lodge in the town of Salines at the house of Signor Pelli, a Venetian merchant.   Reports were brought to him of the brutalities committed by Qarqa Oghlu and his men in the neighbourhood of Famagusta, who were promptly ordered to return to duty at Salines.   They obeyed at once and marched over, leaving that district at peace.

The same day the Pasha invited all the consuls to an audience; they went each by himself, and he enquired from them what was the real state of the island, as though he could not trust anybody's word but theirs.   His conversation with the British consul was longer than the rest, because Mr Turner had taken some part in the negotiations, and was sure to know the ideas of the insurgents, as well as those of the local government.   The next day, the Pasha received in public audience: he allowed his visitors to sit, a condescension on the part of a Pasha.   He then determined to move with all his own troops and those of Qarqa Oghlu towards Nicosia, to begin to give effect to the purposes of his expedition, but he could have wished that the rebels had first retired from the neighbourhood of the capital; for though the united force numbered 2700 men, well equipped and armed, he was afraid of being forced to an engagement with 5000 desperadoes.   He found no better plan than to avail himself of Mr Turner's help, and by him to send a letter into Khalil Agha's camp saying that he wished everyone to retire to his home, and then he would examine quietly the whole matter, to do what was immediately necessary and satisfy all: for he came, he insisted, to bring peace and not war, provided they complied with the reasonable conditions which he would set before them and the government. These expressions, and a panic which spread in the rebel camp, scattered most of the partisans of Khalil Agha; who finding himself left with scarcely 200 of his most devoted followers fled to the fort of Cerines. A good many women also took refuge there, and they prepared for a resolute defence.

This news was conveyed to him by Mr Turner, and forthwith, on July 2, the Pasha marched off his troops to Nicosia, leaving Meleky Bey, captain of the Turkish war vessel, to guard Larnaca with his men, to see that the town was quiet and orderly, and the people free from anxiety.

Qarqa Oghlu, a restless and turbulent spirit, with his savage and barbarous followers, had been guilty of fresh outrages at Salines, for which both the chief and his men had been rebuked and threatened by the Pasha. Thereon they conceived a bitter hatred towards the inhabitants of both towns, and boasted that they would sack every house in Larnaca and Salines, Greek, Turkish and European, and kill the consuls and their *protégés*. This was not pleasant hearing, but no fear was felt as long as the Pasha was in Larnaca. He knew the ruffianly temper of Qarqa Oghlu, and managed to send him off before daylight to Nicosia, and so get him out of places with which he chose to be enraged. Four hours after Mohammad Bey had left the town a villager brought a story that Qarqa Oghlu and his band had met him somewhere off the main road, and had threatened that when the Pasha had passed on he meant to return that very night to Larnaca to ravage the place with fire and sword. His tale was believed, and the whole town was thrown into alarm: some were crying; some flying, some hurriedly burying their treasures in the ground. The European merchants tried to place their books in safety, and to pack up their more valuable possessions to send them on board some vessel. The Turkish, Greek and European women looked despairingly for some hiding place: night was approaching, and with it they expected the arrival of the barbarous Caramanians. It was proposed that they should seek shelter on board ship, and they flocked in troops to the sea shore; but here they found a difficulty, for Meleky Bey, who was on guard at the pier, allowed women only to embark, saying that his honour was at stake, and that he, his men and even the Europeans ought all to be soldiers, and defend each other against such a rebel as Qarqa Oghlu. He tried however to console the crowd by assuring them that he did not for a moment believe the news to be true, and he caused the peasant who had spread it to be sought out and imprisoned. The women would not embark alone, for there was a Turkish man of war in the roadstead, and the licentiousness of Turkish sailors was a byword throughout the Levant. They resolved to retire to the houses of the consuls, which were now armed and guarded by a picket from the man of war. The night was an anxious one, but with morning came the news of the arrival in Nicosia of the Pasha and Qarqa Oghlu, and all was quiet again. The peasant persisted that his story was true. He was brought out of prison, received 100 blows on the soles of his feet and was discharged.

The tranquillity of Larnaca was now assured, and the war vessel went round to the north coast, and lay off the fort at Cerines, where there were already the frigate of Captain Ja'far Bey, a xebec and two galliots, besides two small galliots under Ibrahim Bey, which prevented anyone leaving Cerines, and the fort from receiving help.

The Pasha sent several times from Nicosia to recall Khalil Agha to his duty, bidding him surrender the fort; but seeing these gentle measures had no effect, on July 28 he marched with all his troops to besiege the fort, and began by filling up the ditches with a view to an escalade; but the resistance of those within was stout and effectual, and their guns killed many of the Pasha's soldiers.

The warship landed some cannon to batter the fort, but there were not enough to make any impression on a building so strong, and so well provided with ammunition and food. Force had failed, and the Pasha turned to fraud, but to Meleky Bey alone was reserved the glory of entrapping Khalil Agha.

He pretended to desire a private interview with the rebel chief, which was promised for the night of August 14, when he persuaded Khalil Agha to escape from the fort by a secret way which led down to the sea, and to take refuge on his ship, assuring him of his safety, for his men would never allow him to be carried off; for it was a point of honour with them never to give up a man who sought shelter among them, a point which they would maintain even against their own commander. It was not so in the case of Khalil Agha, who was taken on shore the next day, and handed over to the Pasha, who began by treating him well, giving him a tent to himself, where he was strictly guarded.   Its chief gone, the fort surrendered the same day.   The women were allowed their liberty and their goods.   The men were all kept under guard, the leading insurgents being put in chains, for all Khalil Agha's most devoted adherents had retired with him into the castle.   The fort was now in the Pasha's hands, and on the 19th he caused Khalil Agha to be brought again before him, questioned him at length to discover the other leaders of the revolt, reproved him for his infidelity to the sovereign who had confided to him so important a stronghold and had him strangled in his presence.

All the forts in the kingdom saluted the rebel's death with their guns.   On the 21st before starting on his return to Nicosia the Pasha saw that Qarqa Oghlu and his men were embarked for Caramania, so that they should not have occasion to return through Larnaca.   He then looked to the punishment of the insurgents, 200 of whom were beheaded.   Their heads, with that of their chief, were sent to Constantinople. Peace at last was restored to the island, but not its wealth and well being, which were greatly in decline.

On September 8 the Pasha received from the Porte his third tail, as a recompense for having suppressed the insurrection—an exalted and highly valued distinction.

On October 11 Hafiz Mohammad Efendi, the former

governor, laid down his office, and came to Larnaca, and on the 17th sailed for Constantinople on a Tuscan *polacca* commanded by Captain Tagliagambe.   On the 28th Kior Mohammad Pasha left Nicosia for Cerines, and on the 30th embarked on the small French barque of Captain Vianet, to take up his new *Pashaliq* or government of Koniah.   His troops had already preceded him.   Suleiman Efendi, who is still Governor, took over the administration of the island, his term of office being extended for another year.

This beautiful but unhappy island will never recover from the troubles which have beset her these many years as long as she is governed by the man who pays the Grand Vezir most for the post.

CHAPTER XXI.

ON THE COMMERCE OF THE ISLAND OF CYPRUS.

CYPRUS supplies to European and local commerce produce
of two kinds; the first is natural, consisting of all that is
grown in the island, the second adventitious, consisting of
goods imported from the adjacent shores of Caramania.

Among natural products the chief is cotton, reckoned the
finest in the Levant, for its whiteness, substance and length
of staple. The price it commands in Europe shows its
superiority. The whole crop is not of course of one quality,
but is divided yearly into four kinds, the flower of the crop,
thoroughly saleable, indifferent, and saleable: but when these
four are mingled in due proportion the price is not affected.
By due proportion is understood a mixture which to every ten
bales would allow three of the flower, five of thoroughly
saleable, one of indifferent, and one of saleable. A fifth kind
might be added called sweepings (*scorazze*), which is the
coarsest of all; it is not exported, but used for the common
stuffs of the country.

Cotton is of two kinds, one is produced in village lands
irrigated by streams or torrents, this is the finer kind, and in
greatest request: the other is grown on land which is watered
only by the winter rains.

They begin to sow the seed in April: they might do so
earlier, but then the blade would appear just when the locusts

begin their ravages: the young shoots would be devoured, and they would be obliged to sow over again. Hence the delay. They prepare the soil for sowing cotton just as we prepare our cornfields in Tuscany, and sow the seeds, three or four together, in holes at equal intervals, burying them in the furrow like beans. As soon as the plants are above ground they keep the strongest and pull up the rest. In June and July they hoe lightly round the plants, and root out all the weeds between them. The crop is gathered in October and November, but it requires time to free the cotton from the husk, and extract the seed, so that the first shipments are not ready until the February or March following.

A good crop is reckoned at 5000 bales; sometimes it hardly reaches 3000. Not more than 50 years ago, according to the accounts of persons still alive, it was 8000: and when the island was under Venetian rule it reached 30,000. The difference is to be ascribed to the disproportion of the inhabitants to the cultivable lands: to which may be added two natural causes, want of rain, and the strong hot winds of July, which beat out the cotton just as it is passing from flower to fruit.

The merchants who accept commissions from Europe for this produce base upon them the sums which they advance to their clients, or to the peasants who raise the crop. This is a newly adopted custom, and due to the increase in the number of trading houses: formerly cotton was paid for upon delivery. Bales of cotton usually weigh one cantar of 100 rotoli, the rotolo being equal to $6\frac{3}{4}$ pounds of Florence.

In Cyprus every sort of merchandise, imported or exported, is subject to charges of two kinds. First those of tariff, which are invariable, based upon ancient use and the assent of merchants in Europe; these are reckoned at so much a bale, package, cask, &c. The second charge follows the value of the goods: the Customs take three per centum, the consulate two, brokerage one p.c. on the first cost, commission two p.c. on the cost and expenses. Further if the Cypriot correspondent has had to get bills of exchange on some foreign town, generally Constantinople, he adds one p.c. commission to meet expenses on the bill. The tariff charges will be noticed as we speak of each kind of produce; the other charges may be taken to follow the rules given above.

Cotton exported to Europe pays on each bale tariff at 5 piastres Turkish, or 18⅓ Tuscan lire. We shall reckon the Levant piastre at 3⅔ lire; the oke weight at 3¾ Florentine pounds, the rotolo at 6¼ pounds.

The greater part of the cotton crop is sent to Venice, whence Germany draws its quantum. It fetches so good a price there that a great many English and Dutch houses, as well as merchants in Constantinople and Aleppo, give orders for Cypriot cotton to be consigned to Venice and sold there on their account. Some goes every year by way of Venice to France and Tuscany, and to England and Holland direct.

The second most important article of produce is silk. In May it is all wound off and ready for shipment. The silkworm is treated just as in Tuscany, but runs less risk from the uncertainty of the weather which in the Cypriot spring is more settled. The quality of the silk varies with the places where it is spun: the finest and whitest comes from Famagusta and the Carpasso, that of a lemon or sulphur hue from Citerea and the villages on the same side of the northern range, the golden yellow or orange cocoons from villages in the district of Paphos. The white is most esteemed in Europe, but bales, except those consigned to England, Holland and France occasionally contain lemon or sulphur coloured silk. Venice and Leghorn accept hues equally: white is certainly preferred, but not so exclusively as in the countries farther north. The orange silk is generally bought by the Turks, who pay a piastre more for it, and send it to Cairo, where the colour is much admired, and the thread too is finer.

C. M. T.

One year with another the island produces 25,000 okes of silk. By an old custom the price for the year was fixed at Famagusta at the fair of St Barnabas. The fair continues, but little business is done in silk, and the price follows the crop and the demand. Silk is brought and delivered as it comes from the villages, but is cleaned before it is sent to Europe. The loss is generally from 12 to 15 p.c., which is borne by the European houses on whose account it is purchased. The refuse remains with the agent, who passes it to his principal's credit at a piastre the oke, and gives him an exact account of the loss of weight in cleaning. A bale usually contains 100 okes of clean silk : the tariff charges are 8½ piastres the bale. Constantinople and Aleppo send commissions to Cyprus for silk to be sold in Europe. Some too is shipped for Cairo, *via* Damiata : what is not taken up by the Egyptian factories is sent on from Alexandria to Leghorn, Marseille and Venice. The refuse is generally sent to Cairo, but a small quantity also to Europe. The tariff charges are 2½ piastres the bale of about 60 okes.

Cypriots begin to shear their sheep on March 20, and the wool is exposed for sale in April. Five hundred bales make an average yield, the bale weighing one cantar of 100 rotoli. The rotolo should be 6¾ lbs., but in the case of wool it is hardly 6 lbs. the greasy matter being rapidly absorbed by the sun and air. The white wool is more in request than the dark or black, which is distributed through the bales. Wool is sent to France, but most of it to Leghorn. The tariff charges are 3½ piastres the bale. Shippers have to be careful that the wool has not been exposed to rain or damp. Stowed in a wet state it is very liable to heat, take fire, and destroy the vessel.

Another very important item in the commerce of the island is the wine called Commanderia. The fruit is gathered in August and September ; the grape is red, and the vines small and low. The wine when first made has a rich colour, rather like that of our Chianti. It is put into jars or vessels, pointed below, each of which contains from 15 to 20 of our Tuscan barrels: these are buried up to the middle in the earth, and pitched within to prevent the earth from drawing the wine, hence Cypriot wine commonly tastes of pitch. After a year it begins to lose its redness, and to incline to yellow, and the older it gets the lighter it becomes, so that wine of eight or ten years old resembles in colour our muscadine. During the change the lees (called in Cyprus the *mother* of the wine) settle in great quantity. These give body to the wine, and are never taken out, unless it be to transfer them from one jar to another.

Bargains are struck in the villages, at so much the load, each load being composed of sixteen κούζαι, and each κούζα of five Florentine flasks. When the wine comes from the country into the town it should be run into casks in which are lees: and provided it stay at least a year in each cask, it gains by being transferred from cask to cask. The casks may be nearly full or half full, and the wine will not suffer, but a space of half a palm should be left empty at the top.

The villager who sells the wine must see that it maintains its condition, whether it remains in his hands or is stored by the purchaser, up to August 15 (O.S.) next after the vintage. On that day it is examined, if it is spoiled the seller must take it back, if it is good it is charged to the buyer, for after the first year it is not subject to deterioration.

The island produces annually 40,000 couzai of wine. The whole crop takes its name from the "Commandery," which hardly supplies 10,000 couzai, but of the best quality. The rest comes from different parts of the island. Most of it is exported to Venice, where, even in the cafés, it is largely drunk. But the Venetians are not very particular about the quality, never buying wine more than 18 months old, and paying only a piastre the couza. The older or finer quality is sent to France, Holland and Tuscany, and costs from 2½ to

3 piastres the couza. Of late a considerable quantity of the commoner wine has gone to Leghorn. It is exported in casks of 70 couzai: the tariff charges, including the value of the cask, amount to $10\frac{3}{4}$ piastres. The oldest wines in the market are eight or ten years old: it is not true as some people in Europe think, that one can find it of a hundred. It is customary however on the birth of a child for the father to bury a jar full of wine well sealed, which is kept until the day of his or her marriage, when it is served at the wedding feast, and distributed among relations and friends. This is the oldest wine one can find, and would be 20 years old or a little more; but it is never sold, being kept for presents.

The island produces other wines, used at meals, not unlike those of Provence. The best is made in the village of Omodos. It is originally dark, but after a few years begins to turn yellow, and in colour and taste to grow like that of the Commandery. It is not exported, but drunk in the island, and on the vessels which trade with the coast of Syria. The muscadine wines make up scarcely 5000 couzai. The price is the same as that of the Commandery, and the tariff charges the same. The development of the two kinds is quite different. The muscadine in the first year is a little lighter than ours: with age it acquires a rich red colour, and great body, with such sweetness that it is generally better liked when only one or two years old.

Colocynth is a plant of the gourd kind. It creeps along the ground like a cucumber, which it resembles greatly in the leaf and flower: and in the fruit too, when the cucumber is no bigger than an apple, which is the size of the largest colocynth. Freshly gathered it is dark green with yellow stripes. It is set to dry under a strong sun, and becomes entirely yellow: the rind, which is useless, is stripped off, and there remains a pulp, full of seeds: these also are of no use. The plant generally grows wild, and is seen over great tracts of country: yet it is difficult to collect yearly 100 cantars of 100 rotoli each, so light is it when stripped and dried. It is gathered in May.

The largest orders come from Amsterdam, Hamburg and Leghorn; some few from Marseille and Venice. It is packed in large cases, containing a cantar or half a cantar. Colocynth is most valuable when, the outer husk being stripped off, it remains white and whole. Great care is therefore used in the packing, but some of it is always broken. The quality is not impaired, but the European buyer suffers a loss, because the seed which falls out is credited by custom to the seller, and as that is the heaviest part the loss of it may reduce the weight of the consignment by 50 p.c. The pulp only is sent to England, the seed being extracted: so English merchants who buy but a small quantity, export it in sacks, not caring if it be broken or not. Water and even damp ruin it utterly. Tariff charges to Leghorn amount to $15\frac{1}{4}$ piastres the cantar, and $10\frac{1}{4}$ the half cantar, including the value of the case.

Ladanum is gathered in spring, chiefly in the village of Lefcara. It is a kind of dew, which falls at night on a plant very like the small *salvia*, whose flower resembles the wild rose of our hedges. Early in the morning before the sun has absorbed this dew the shepherds lead their goats to feed where this plant is found. The ladanum is then soft and viscous, and sticks to their beards, from which it is picked: this is the purest kind. While the goats are grazing the shepherds too are engaged in collecting the stuff with a short stick at the end of which are fastened strips of goat's skin, which they trail over the plants. As the wind rises it sprinkles the flowers with dust, and the ladanum is more or less mixed with earth. But it is cleaned with oil and fire, making it softer and more pliant, and of sweeter smell. It is usually sent to Nicosia to be cleaned and packed, and despatched from Larnaca to all parts of Europe. Tariff charges for Leghorn amount to $5\frac{3}{4}$ piastres the box, weighing from 60 to 100 okes.

Madder is a root which furnishes a red dye, grown in the

fields near the sea at Famagusta and Citti on sandy and stony soil. It is of two sorts, one which springs of itself, the other from seed sown. To get a large crop of madder it must be dug every second or third year, the root is then thicker and richer in colouring matter: if gathered every year it is small poor stuff, with little of the pulp in which the colour is secreted. This is the outer coat or rind, the inside is a thin fibrous substance which yields no dye.

The root may be dug at any time of the year, but as it lies very deep in the ground it is generally collected in January and February, when the rains have softened the soil. After extracting the root the holes are filled in again, and bits which remain propagate and spread, so that in two years the same quantity is found again, or even more if the winter has been unusually wet. As soon as it is dug up the root is set to dry, but not directly in the sun, which would affect the colour. Madder was formerly a capital article of commerce with Aleppo and Baghdad, whence it passed into Persia. But since the disturbances in that country, where arts and trade are on the decline, very little is sent there; but a new trade has been opened with France, which takes, either directly or through Leghorn, the largest part of the crop. In the Levant cotton stuffs are dyed red with a mixture made from this root and sheep's blood. The tariff charges on madder are 5 piastres the cantar of 100 rotoli. The bales, like those of wool, must be thoroughly dry, or they are likely to catch fire on board.

Cochineal is exported to Venice: the quality is small, but the profit considerable. Tariff charges are $6\frac{1}{2}$ piastres the bag of 200 okes.

Soda (*Salsola*) grows at Calopsidia; the plant is burnt and yields an ash which is used to make soap and glass. The burning is carried out in summer, and in September and October the ash is ready for export. While I was in Cyprus I only knew it sent to Marseille. The tariff charges are $\frac{3}{4}$ piastre the bag.

Turpentine is gathered in Cyprus of two qualities: the first and most perfect is that which oozes in clear drops from incisions made in the *Pistacia terebinthus*, and is gathered thence in the summer mornings. The lower quality is that which has trickled down to the ground, and is less clean. Both kinds are exported in jars containing 20 pounds each. Buyers must be extremely wary, and not trust to the excellent appearance of the turpentine on the top, for the villagers are often dishonest enough to fill the lower part of the jar with the poorer stuff. Cyprus turpentine has a great reputation, especially at Venice. It is collected chiefly in the district of Pafo. The tariff charges are $4\frac{1}{4}$ piastres the case of four jars.

Woven stuffs are of two kinds, either of silk and cotton mixed, or of cotton only. The trade in these with Europe used to be extensive, but for some years past the enhanced price of cotton has restricted the export to the stuffs called *rasetti*, and others in which silk and cotton are mixed. Nicosia is the chief seat of the trade: the tariff charges are 3 piastres a box, the contents of which may have a value of 500 piastres.

Green earth is used by painters. The fixed price is $4\frac{1}{2}$ piastres the cantar of 100 rotoli. It is brought from the pit in baskets made of palm leaves; three of these make a cantar. It is sent largely to Holland, often as ballast. The tariff charges are $1\frac{1}{5}$ piastre the cantar.

Umber is found of the finest quality. It costs nothing beyond the carriage from the pits at $1\frac{1}{4}$ piastre the cartload of about 1200 lbs. Tariff charges are $\frac{3}{4}$ piastre. Most of it goes to Holland.

Grain is produced in Cyprus beyond the wants of its inhabitants, so that there is opportunity of exporting several cargoes every year. But it is to be observed that though the government of the island may allow the export, vessels carrying grain are always liable to meet an Ottoman man of war, when the cargo would be confiscated, as the Porte does not allow the export of food stuffs from its own territories to those of France and Italy, or to any other country not under its rule.   Vessels however carry every year large quantities of grain to Leghorn, Genoa, Marseille and Malta.   The licenses obtained from the several Governors are never issued for Christian countries, but for other ports in the Turkish dominions.   The destination of the vessels is well known, but officials take the customary dues, and let them sail.   In the same way the Ottoman men of war which meet a vessel charged with grain, which they know is bound to a European port, take a handful of sequins and let it go its way.   For the commanders would gain nothing by taking it to Constantinople, where the vessel would suffer no loss beyond the confiscation of the cargo, which would go into the Imperial barns.   The ambassadors of Christian Powers accredited to the Porte have now and then successfully opposed these exactions, and obtained cash payments for cargoes so seized.   Only a few years since, Mons. de Penklern, Internuncio of their Imperial Majesties, obtained restitution of the value of a cargo of wheat, loaded for Leghorn on a Tuscan *polacca*, and seized by a Turkish war vessel for the use of the Sultan.   A merchant who proposes to ship grain from Cyprus should obtain through his consul a license from the Governor at Nicosia, which will cost $1\frac{3}{8}$ piastre for the *mosa* of three Florentine sacks.   This payment is included in the tariff charges which I shall note below.

The wheat grown in the eastern parts of Cyprus is of good quality, but does not keep and is consumed year by year in the island itself.   The wheat of other districts is finer, heavier, and keeps better: the best of all comes from the district of Pafo and Fontana Amorosa, and this is exported to Europe.   It would be well if we in Italy were better informed about this produce.   Of late years the market of Leghorn has received several cargoes from Pafo and Fontana Amorosa which met with so bad a reception that merchants there would never again accept or order wheat from Cyprus, on the plea that it is of bad quality, and unwholesome on account of all kinds of seeds improperly mixed in it.

Persons who have seen the bread made in the island from this very grain, and even from that grown in the rest of the island, have found it not only of excellent quality, but the best and finest you would get throughout Syria and other parts of the Levant.   It owes this pre-eminence to the diligence and address of the women, who pick over the wheat very carefully, and take out the grains which would make the bread brownish, but these do not exist in the proportion which some suppose. Even after cleaning it thus they wash it, and reject the grains which have been eaten out by weevil, an easy task, because they float on the water in which they are washed.   They never remit their care even in times of famine : thinking, very reasonably, that the loss is hardly felt, while no grinding can make the empty grain into flour, but mere bran ; and lastly that they assure their health by cleaning the wheat, and getting rid of other seeds and of earth, which gives no nourishment, and is even very hurtful.

Wheat is measured in Cyprus by the *mosa* of three Florentine sacks.   Tariff charges are $1\frac{1}{4}$ piastre the *mosa* including brokerage.   Note that in wheat transactions the Tuscan consulate takes only two p. c. on a value of 2 piastres the *mosa* : and the Customs take 28 piastres the 100 *mosa*, instead of three p.c.

Barley throughout the island is of excellent quality.   It is chiefly sent through European merchants to the coast of Syria.   A license from the Governor, obtained through the consul, is necessary for the export.   This costs $\frac{3}{4}$ piastre the *mosa*, and the tariff charges, including this, are $\frac{7}{8}$ piastre the *mosa*.   Nothing further is payable to the Customs, the consulate or the broker : only the commission at four p.c. on the cost and expenses.

The salt extracted from the natural salines of the island

is no longer an article of trade with Europe; probably vessels do not find it worth their while to take it. I may mention however that the fixed value is $3\frac{3}{8}$ piastres the cartload of 1000 okes. Tariff charges are hardly a piastre. Salt is exported now to Syria and Constantinople only. Masters of vessels loading for Syria take it on their own account, and sell it themselves. The voyages are short, and not unprofitable. But ships destined for Constantinople only take salt when they cannot find more valuable cargo.

Carobs, pitch, tar and planks are other articles of export. Carobs especially are important to the native traders, Turk and Greek, who send them to Alexandria. Many of the European vessels engaged in the Levant trade are employed in transporting this produce. The other three articles make but an insignificant figure. European merchants leave them to the natives.

The natural products are thus shown to be the staples of Cypriot commerce, but I must mention a few things which come from Caramania to be re-exported to Europe.

Storax is brought over in small boxes. It is considered perfect when it is quite pure, and has a large proportion of white grains. Buyers try the boxes with a knife, for they always contain a surface layer of fine white grains, far superior to the bulk of the storax below. This is a common practice, and allowed for in the bargain. It is sent to all parts of Europe. Tariff charges are $1\frac{3}{4}$ piastre the case of four boxes, each containing from 30 to 33 Florentine pounds of pure storax.

By scraping the incisions in the tree from which the pure storax exudes, another kind is collected called *Storax calamita*. With this they mix the gum which trickles down naturally from the tree, even when it is soiled with the earth at the foot. They carry this to Cyprus, and put it over the fire in large caldrons, and by continually stirring they separate the earth and the coarser scrapings: these, called *semola di storace*, they sell extremely cheaply, for the oily matter is almost lost. Thus cleaned and put into bags the *Storax calamita* is sold to European merchants, who send it to various western countries. Tariff charges are 2½ piastres the sack of 50 to 60 okes. The best kind is rich in oil, and darkish in colour. It is judged by working it up in the fingers to note its cohesiveness, and lighting it to see how slowly it consumes. The better qualities should stand both these tests.

Camel's hair, which is brought to Cyprus from Caramania, is of the same kind as that exported to Europe from Smyrna, but the former is less clean, and is full of bristles (called *mostacci*) which are useless, and at Smyrna are picked out. The same care might be taken in Cyprus, but where the inhabitants are so few they will not address themselves to a work which requires care and time. However the trade began some few years since, and though the European demand is small, the low price serves to sell this produce. Tariff charges are 3¼ piastres the bale of 100 okes.

Yellow wax is chiefly sold at Nicosia, and sent thence to Larnaca, to be exported in casks or bales of 100 okes each. Tariff charges are 5½ piastres the bale.

Gall nuts, used by dyers, are grown in Caramania. There are several kinds, the best is the *Galla spinosa*, so called from the spines scattered over each nut. The nuts are dark green or nearly black, and heavy. Another variety is yellowish, but these have not the active properties of the darker nuts. Very few of these pass through Cyprus, most of them are sold at Smyrna and Aleppo for export to Europe. The best are grown in the neighbourhood of Mosul on the Tigris, and exported from Aleppo. Those which reach Cyprus from Caramania are not the *Galla spinosa*: they are light in weight, yellow, and altogether of inferior quality. They are in small demand in Europe, except in years when the *Galla spinosa* is very scarce and dear. Tariff charges amount to 3½ piastres the bag.

To this enumeration of the exports from the island I ought

to add an account of the imports. But these are really of very
small consequence, because Cyprus imports only just enough
for the wants of its own scanty inhabitants. I may say
however that there is a yearly consumption of 25 bales of the
fine French cloth called *londrins* of the second quality: two
cases, each of 10 pieces, of satins of Florentine or Russian
make: four cases of Lucca satins, of all colours except black
and green: one case of various light stuffs. Twenty barrels of
tin, 20 bags of pepper, 100 cantars of iron, the Tuscan being
preferred: 100 cantars of lead, 200 okes of American indigo,
100 okes of cochineal: the profits on these being generally
from 15 to 20 p.c. A quite insignificant quantity of the
same articles is imported for the use of the countries in the
Levant.

Payments are made in cash or bills of exchange. The bills
current in Cyprus are always those issued in Constantinople
either by order and on account of foreign correspondents, or
by endorsement of negotiable drafts. Such negotiations are
chiefly arranged with the island government, the consular
dragomans being the exchange brokers, and receiving ½ p.c.,
paid according to custom by the drawer. Bills on Constantinople are generally payable at 31 days date and payment
is made in two instalments, half upon the negotiation of the
bills, the other half 31 days later. One p. c. is charged
against the correspondent for brokerage and commission.

Interest is reckoned in Cyprus at 12 p.c. per annum. The
rate is of old standing, and generally allowed in consideration of the great risk which attends the lending of money
to villagers. The law of Mohammad confounds usury with
loans on interest, so that both are forbidden to Turks. Nevertheless they lend and borrow, but in notes of hand the
lender includes the interest with the principal; thus a loan
of 100 piastres would be entered on the bond as 112 piastres
without further note. The only coins current in the island are
those which bear the Sultan's cypher, and Venetian sequins.

I will end this chapter by noting that every year about 600 merchant vessels touch at Cyprus, under the flags of various European nations. These sail in small squadrons, either to transport passengers and merchandise from one part of Syria to another, or to trade with Europe. A still larger number of ships of all kinds come under the Ottoman flag, as well as the Sultan's war vessels, and those of other sovereigns. While I was living in the island there came, in 1761, one Venetian ship and two frigates, commanded by Sr Foscari, and one ship by Sr Alvise Riva; in 1762, one Venetian ship and one frigate commanded by Sr Foscari: two French ships, one frigate and two xebecs commanded by M. de Bon; in 1763, one Venetian frigate commanded by Sr Molino; in 1766, one French ship and two frigates commanded by M. de Beauffremont, Prince de Listenois, and one Venetian frigate under Sr Zeno.

The principal object of the visits paid by men of war to the very furthest ports in the Levant is to see how mercantile houses are carried on, and to correct abuses which may have arisen, as well as to give greater importance to the subjects of their several sovereigns established in the east. The Turks are deeply impressed by the presence in their waters of the war vessels of Christian princes.

CHAPTER XXII.

OF THE CONSULS OF EUROPEAN SOVEREIGNS, AND OF THEIR FUNCTIONS IN THE ISLAND OF CYPRUS, AND IN OTHER PORTS OF SYRIA.

THE consul of France, now M. Benoit Astier, an esquire and privy councillor, has in all circumstances, public and private, precedence over his colleagues. He is bound to protect all the subjects of his most Christian Majesty, as well as other Europeans not specially commended to the protection of another Power. These last however may choose what Power they will, but the Genoese generally choose that of France. His officials are these: the Deputy of the colony, who is also Treasurer, and is elected yearly from the French merchants. He acts in the absence of the consul.

The chancellor of the consulate holds his office under a royal patent, and, as well as the consul, may wear a sword. After him come the first, second and the third dragomans or interpreters.

The authority of the French consul is wider than that of the others. He can command *de par le Roi*, and such commands must be obeyed. To debate on any national question he assembles the merchants in his office, and the matter is decided by a majority of votes.

Mr Timothy Turner, the English consul, died in 1768, while I was writing this work. He was an officer of the Levant Company; but held a commission from His Britannic Majesty.

Under commissions from their several embassies at Constantinople he acted as vice-consul for the Empire, Tuscany,
Denmark and Holland. The authority of the English consul
is not so large as that of his French colleague. He can inflict
trifling punishments, but he cannot at once banish his *protégés*,
except when some very grave crime would injure the repute of
his nation in the eyes of the local government; or when
he knows that one of his subjects is about to embrace the
Mohammadan faith. In these cases he can examine the
matter, and put the accused under restraint until an opportunity
comes of sending him back to Europe. The English consulate
has an English chancellor, approved by the Levant Company,
as well as a Tuscan chancellor, approved by the Imperial
Internuncio at Constantinople, who is at the service of the
Imperial and Tuscan subjects, while Dutchmen and Danes
avail themselves of the help of the English chancellor. The
English dragoman is paid by the Levant Company, but receives
from the consul further remuneration for his services to the
other consular *protégés*.

Until quite lately Neapolitans had a consul of their own,
but his duties are now discharged by the Venetian consul.
The Venetian consul, now Signor Bernardo Caprara, has
jurisdiction not only in Cyprus but over the coast of Syria
from Jaffa to Tripoli; to these ports he appoints vice-consuls.
He protects Neapolitans and Sicilians under letters patent
from the Neapolitan ambassador at Constantinople: and the
Swedes in the same way. His chancellor must be a native of
Venice, and is paid by the republic. The dragoman is paid
by the consul.

Four or five years ago there was also a consul for Ragusa,
but after the departure of Signor Francesco Sodarnia the post
was not filled up, though there are several merchants of that
republic. One of these undertakes the duties of the consulate,
though bills of health are signed by the French consul.

On the arrival of a new consul in the roadstead of Larnaca,

he sends at once to inform his subjects, and whoever may be acting as vice-consul sends his dragoman to inform the other consuls. These hoist their several ensigns, and at the hour appointed for the landing send their chancellor, dragoman and Janissaries to receive him on the shore. The subjects of the new consul are assembled there, and all escort him to his house, where the dragomans offer him the usual compliments. (Consuls hold, besides the letters patent of their own sovereign, the *berat* or exequatur of the Porte, in which they are styled *beyler-bey*, a title equal to ambassador.) The first dragoman is despatched at once to the capital to inform the government of his arrival, and of the double authority under which he assumes his office. The Governor dismisses the dragoman with congratulations, and on the latter's return the letters patent are read and the consul takes official possession of his post. The other consuls pay him visits of compliment, which he returns with the same ceremony.

The regular expenses of a consulate consist of the presents offered at certain set times to local officials, amounting yearly to 400 Turkish piastres or 100 Florentine sequins, and the expenses of dragomans and Janissaries 100 sequins more. Extraordinary expenses are those incurred on behalf of a subject who, for the honour of the nation, has to be ransomed from the hands of the local police, and cannot himself pay the sum required. Or again on the visit of a Pasha, when the present offered him in stuffs and cloth costs as much as 150 sequins. Presents too are made to the commanders of caravels, or Turkish men of war, which anchor in the roadstead.

The captains and officers of men of war are entitled to board at the table of their consul. The French consul is allowed 10 piastres or $2\frac{1}{2}$ sequins a day for each such vessel. The English consul keeps an account of his expenses and forwards it to the Levant Company, by whom he is repaid, with some slight addition. The Venetian consul bears his own charges.

One of the chief duties of a consul in Turkey is to enhance as much as possible the dignity of the sovereign whom he represents, and to protect to the best of his power not only his subjects, but others commended to his care. A consul must not protect the subject of any Prince who is represented in the same city by a consul of his own, but he may give refuge to anyone who escapes from the jurisdiction of his own consulate, the consular house being inviolable, even by the Turks.

He has no right whatever to protect one of the *ri'aya*, or Christian subjects of the Porte, unless by virtue of a *Berat* from the Porte, and the letters patent of the ambassador in Constantinople of the sovereign whose protection is claimed. In 1766 this order was republished in Cyprus by a *Khatti Humayun*, or Imperial Rescript. On that occasion the Governor, Suleiman Efendi, upon receiving this document, wrote to the consuls at Larnaca to say that he was ordered to communicate it to them, and desired them to send their dragomans to Nicosia to hear it read. The consuls replied with one voice that their residence was at Larnaca, and that the Khatti Humayun should be sent to be read in the presence of their dragomans in the court there. Suleiman Efendi was impressed by their vigorous unanimity, and thought it best to yield, and in future to treat the representatives of Christian Princes with more consideration. The Rescript was sent to Larnaca and read there, and the dragomans, on behalf of their consuls, assured the Government that its just provisions would be duly respected. As they had never contravened it, they had no occasion to say more.

Consuls can arrange differences which arise between their own subjects or *protégés*, and even (with the consent of their colleague) between these and subjects of another Power. Arbiters are appointed to hear the case, but the parties cannot be forced into an arrangement, and are free to carry the matter before any competent European court.

If a new Governor lands at Cerines, on his arrival at

C. M. T. 9

Nicosia each consul must send thither a dragoman and a janissary to offer the usual compliments. If he lands at Salines, he is greeted there, and again at Nicosia. It may happen that the Governor wishes to receive the consuls and their colony, in such case he appoints a day. He never returns these visits, but neither can he expect them, unless he chances to be at Larnaca. Should any Pasha happen to touch at Larnaca the consuls must send their dragomans and janissaries to compliment him on board. If he lands and invites them to call upon him, they do so with the ceremony used to a Governor, but their visit is not returned. When a *Digdaban* or Commissioner comes to take up the post of Governor of Larnaca, or a *Qazi* is installed, they are the first to call upon the consuls, who receive them in state, and later return the visit.

If a son is born to the Sultan, and the local government holds public rejoicings, the consuls also illuminate their houses for three days, and keep open a room in which coffee is offered to anyone, Moslem or Christian, who comes there. I assisted at one of these feasts in January, 1762, which was distinguished by fireworks and dances. The national ensign is hoisted, and dragomans and janissaries are sent to Nicosia to congratulate the Governor.

Besides the compliments exchanged between consuls on their arrival in the island, ceremonial visits are paid on the sovereign's birthday, on the arrival of any personage (as an admiral or captain of a man of war) and on New Year's day. In paying visits at private houses the consul is preceded by a janissary only: if he be obliged to take an interpreter, the dragoman must walk by his side, not in front of him, as on public occasions.

It is most necessary that the consuls should exhibit to the public, and to the Turks particularly, an entire unanimity, and a common policy. These inspire respect and even fear, for when the consuls act in harmony, their representations against

some exaction or injustice on the part of the island government
are treated with proper consideration.

In cases of a war between two Powers their representatives
exchange no formal visits. In the last war between England
and France the English consul conducted business with his
French colleague through the Tuscan chancellor and dragoman.
A consul invites his fellow subjects to be present at all official
visits. The formal visits paid by a consul to a Governor or
other high Turkish official are preceded by gifts, of greater
or less value according to the rank of the recipient. In Cyprus
such visits are only paid to the Governor, if he comes to Larnaca,
to the *Digdaban* and *Qazi*, or to any passing Pasha who may
care to accept them.

In the case of the Governor the hour is fixed and a dragoman
and janissary sent to carry the present, which generally consists
of garments of cloth or stuff. Then the consul and his colony
start, preceded by two janissaries wearing *dolmans*, a long red
gown with black trimmings, and the cap called *stemma* on their
heads. After them come the dragomans, then the consul, who
is followed by his colony. An official is deputed to receive
the consul at the door of the Governor's palace, and to conduct
him to the hall of audience, which is lined with *choqadars* and
chawushes. The Governor enters from another room, and the
chawushes shout "ya Allah!" and Arabic phrases meaning
"God save our Master." The consul takes his seat on a chair
which he has sent expressly from his own house, and the
Governor sits on a *divan* or sofa, a kind of couch covered with
printed calico or stuff, and furnished with cushions. The
consul's suite sit on the same sofa at a distance from the
Governor. The other Turks and the servants stand, the
choqadars and *chawushes* round the Governor, in a respectful
attitude, their hands crossed on their breasts and their eyes
fixed on their master, whose least look or sign they understand
and obey. While the first compliments are exchanged neither
the consul nor his suite take off their hats: they press their

hands to the left breast and bow slightly. The Governor extends his hand to the consul, and then raises it to his mouth. After this they ask after the health of their respective sovereigns, and chat about politics and the news; of the day. A *choqadar* then kneels before the Governor and spreads a napkin of some gay colour over his knees: with a bow only he offers another to the consul. They are then served in due order with candied fruits preserved in syrup, then coffee made without sugar and served in cups which are not quite full, a custom which the Turks think more polite: and lastly with a kind of sherbet smelling of musk and amber. The talk continues as long as the Governor pleases: finally one *choqadar* bears a vase of rose water, another a kind of thurible, the first lightly sprinkles the face and hands of the Governor and his guest, the other censes them with burning aloe chips. This is a graceful way of indicating that the audience is over. The consul takes his leave, but the Governor does not rise from his seat. As they leave the palace the guests receive a handkerchief or so of muslin or gauze. The same ceremonial is observed when the consul visits a Pasha, but the Pasha's suite is more numerous, and the consul only is permitted to sit. A band plays during the audience, consisting of kettle drums, cymbals, oboes, reed-flutes, trumpets, hunting horns and psalteries.

The *Digdaban* and *Qazi*, when they take up their duties, the one of Commissioner, the other of Judge, pay the first visit to the consuls. The same ceremonial is applied to both. The officer arranges the hour, and arrives on horseback with three or four *choqadars*. He does not take off his outer boots until he is seated on the divan. The consul receives him standing and covered. They sit down and converse through their interpreters, who stand. A janissary offers the *Digdaban* a pipe, and then candied fruits or sweetmeats, coffee and lemonade, and on his departure rose water and incense. His servants replace his boots, and he takes his leave. The consul remains in the room, but the dragomans conduct the *Digdaban* to the door, walking close to him as though to support his arms. A few days later the visit is returned by the consul and his colony with the same forms as are observed towards a Governor, except that his janissaries do not wear the high cap, but their usual turban. The *Digdaban* or *Qazi* must not keep the consul waiting his entry, as a Governor or Pasha would do.

If the archbishop of Cyprus visits Larnaca he calls first on the consul, who returns his visit with the forms observed towards the Governor.

I may explain that the term *divan* (or sofa) is used in the East of certain parts of the hall raised one or two palms from the ground and covered with rugs: all round are mattresses three *braccia* broad, covered with calico or other stuffs, and against these are set pillows, at least two *braccia* long and one high, also encased in stuff. On these the Turks sit to talk, to eat and often to sleep. The word *divan* means also a council-hall, or room for public meetings.

Consuls in the Levant must watch carefully the state of health in the countries where they reside, and in those adjoining, and on the slightest suspicion of the plague to advise the government which they represent, and to note the fact on the bills of health of vessels sailing for Europe. The least negligence on this point is inexcusable. They must note too on the bills of health when the country is clean, and how long it has been so.

There are now only three consuls in Cyprus. Those of France and Venice, as well as their chancellors, are forbidden to trade. The English consul is in this respect perfectly free.

Upon the death of a consul, chancellor, dragoman or merchant, the consular ensign is hoisted at half mast: notice being sent to the other consuls, who do the same, and with their colonies accompany the funeral to the church. At the funeral of a consul only the janissaries wear their full dress.

Were an archbishop or bishop to die in Larnaca—the Greeks, as I have said before, are all schismatics—in consideration of the position they fill among their own people, the consuls send one of their officers, just as a mark of respect.

CHAPTER XXIII.

OF THE VARIOUS OFFICERS OF THE CONSULATES AND THEIR FUNCTIONS.

THE chancellors of consulates are generally subjects of the Power represented. Their duties are to keep a register of all acts done in the chancery, to examine ships' papers, and to hand them to the captains who sail for Europe, annexing to them their bills of lading and of health. They may extract and seal copies of acts done in the chancery. The consul verifies his chancellor's signature, and his attestation is accepted in the law courts and elsewhere. The chancellors are not doctors of law, but are mere secretaries of the consulates.

Official dragomans are employed and paid to translate the languages of the East either verbally, or from documents. They must be always at the consul's call, and carry his messages to governors or judges. At a public audience, though the consul may speak Eastern languages perfectly, he must invariably address a Turk in his own tongue, and the dragoman must interpret his words. All negotiations, however great their importance, are conducted by a dragoman, who is then accompanied by a janissary. Another kind of dragoman is called *beratli* (*barattaro*) from the *berat* or diploma given him by the Porte. These are always Ottoman subjects, assigned by the Sultan to the several ambassadors and distributed by them among consulates in the Levant. They are Greeks, Armenians and Jews, and their position costs them 500 sequins. On obtaining the *berat* they become the subjects of the Power to which they are allotted, and are exempted from allegiance to the Sultan, and from extortion at the hands of his officers. As long as a *beratli* lives, his wife and children share his privileges, but on his death they become again subjects of the Porte. Their only duty is to treat the consul with due respect as their protector. The consul cannot force one of them to interpret for him, even upon payment. Dragomans dress like Turks, but wear on their heads a *qalpaq*, or tall cap of marten or other skin, instead of the turban.

Janissaries are Turkish soldiers, who stand as guards at the doors of the consular houses, and walk before the consul in the streets, carrying a staff, which they keep striking on the ground, to warn the people to give way. A consul generally has two, and he may choose his own men by an understanding with the *Yenicheri-Agha*. He may even have more if he cares to pay for them.

CHAPTER XXIV.

THE DUTIES OF PROTECTED SUBJECTS IN THE LEVANT: AND THOSE OF MASTERS OF VESSELS ON ARRIVING AT A PORT.

PROTECTED subjects are expected to recognise the consul as their chief, and to pay him due respect, especially in the presence of Ottoman subjects, who are thereby led to give greater importance to the nation which he represents. He must wait upon the consul when summoned by him, and pay him a visit of compliment every New Year's day. The fees due by him are fixed by the Sovereign, and must be loyally paid. The consul can in no way add to them.

Before taking a case into a Turkish court the permission of the consul must be obtained. Differences among themselves, or with the subjects of another Power, which they cannot arrange amicably, must be submitted to the consul's decision.

If a man leaves his ordinary residence, whether to go into the country or travel abroad, he should advise the consul, so that if any disturbance arises, he may get early warning.

A European who wishes to marry informs his consul, who offers no objection if the man be a merchant or able to maintain a wife, and the woman is a European or the *protégée* of a Christian Power. It is expressly forbidden to a European to marry an Ottoman subject: were he to do so he would be liable to pay *kharaj*. The consul could not help him, and would withdraw his protection from both the man and the woman.

A Frenchman is forbidden to marry in the Levant. If he dared to do so, within two months of the publication of such marriage the consul must order the parties to sail for France, and the order must be obeyed.

Everyone is free to trade by wholesale or retail, but the French must be authorised by a certificate of the Chamber of Commerce at Marseille, and after 10 years must return to France. Subjects of other nations can stay as long as they please.

Any European, wherever he may come from is bound to appear before his consul, and explain his reasons for coming. If he turns out to be a mere vagabond the consul is fully furnished with instructions how to get rid of him as soon as possible, and send him back to Europe.

The master of a vessel arriving from abroad must on landing, even before he calls on his correspondents, go to the consul and inform him whence he comes, what is his business, and give him the letters he brings; and a day or two before he leaves he must do the same. He must show the consul his papers: if he makes a difficulty about bringing them ashore the consul sends his chancellor to examine them on board. In Syria, where vessels generally anchor on the beach, the consuls cannot oblige the masters to bring their papers ashore, lest they should be obliged suddenly to hoist sail and leave the shore, for fear of a disaster.

Every ship's captain ought to be fully acquainted with his duties, but mistakes or misdoings have perhaps graver consequences in Turkey than elsewhere; the consuls ought therefore to watch their proceedings very narrowly, to avoid continual complaints from the Turks, in whose service the vessels are chiefly employed for the transport of merchandise, passengers and pilgrims: the misconduct of merchant captains

has often brought discredit to the national flag.   If the custom
of returning to Europe every three years to renew their certi-
ficates were rigorously observed, many inconveniences which
now arise in Syria would be avoided.

A vessel which has plague on board must, on anchoring
in any roadstead or harbour, signal for assistance before
allowing anyone to land.   And although in the Levant the
government employs no precautions of its own, the consuls
will not allow a ship to communicate with the shore unless
there be plague already in the country.

In the year 1765, at a time when Cyprus enjoyed perfect
health, a French vessel lightly laden arrived in a plague stricken
condition from Constantinople : the greater part of the crew
was dead, only three persons remaining on board alive.   The
consul, in the name of the King, forbade these three to land,
prescribing a strict quarantine.   Two of them died : after forty
days *pratique* was given to the survivor, and five days later to
the vessel, to which volunteers had been sent to clean it, and
to spread out the merchandise in the sun.   One of these men
died while shifting the cargo, and it was evident that the
disease was thoroughly rooted in the vessel, and its freight.
All these precautions proved the salvation of Cyprus, where
the health continued perfect ; and no case of plague has
occurred since the outbreak of 1760.

A European vessel which leaves a port in the Levant where
there is plague, although bound for other Turkish ports, must
always take a bill of health ; and if this is foul, the master is
bound on arriving at his destination to inform the consul, if
there be one, before communicating with the shore, and to obey
his orders.

CHAPTER XXV.

ACCOUNT OF THE PLAGUE OF A.D. 1760 IN THE ISLAND OF CYPRUS.

THE contentment inspired by my short and prosperous voyage from Leghorn to Cyprus was turned to bitterness on the very day of my arrival, February 3, 1760, on hearing the disagreeable news that the island was attacked by the plague. The Salines and Larnaca were still free but in great alarm, for in Nicosia the mortality increased every day, and the spread of the disease throughout the island, and first of all in the seaports, as most thickly populated, seemed inevitable. Every consul, merchant and other Europeans were careful with whom they associated. Some had cut themselves off from all persons whatever: some were preparing to shut themselves up in their houses, before the plague spread further, and so to accustom themselves to a voluntary prison until God were pleased to take the curse off the land. I was far more timorous when I saw the scourge so near me, than when I watched its ravages from afar. However the next day I was bound to land, and was warned by a European gentleman to be very careful not to touch any person, nor any thing which was susceptible of the infection, although he assured me that neither in the town of Salines, nor in Larnaca, was there any case of plague, but that the frequent communication with Nicosia made everyone anxious.

As I set out, as in duty bound, for the consul's house,

I observed that people were no less anxious to avoid contact with me than I with them. The consul received me kindly, and knowing that I came from an uninfected country invited me to dinner. The French consul did the same; the other consuls were already shut up, and most of the merchants would have no communication with the outer world. The same evening, on going to take leave of my own consul, I found him about to take stricter precautions, as he had heard that three persons in Salines were attacked. I returned to sleep on board.

Next day I landed to pay my respects to the French consul, and was at once warned that of the three persons attacked two were dead, and the third was dangerously ill. Other persons too had been seized. I went straight to my own consul, who had cut himself completely off and I could only talk with him through the grating or barrier which on such occasions is put across the door. I found the French consul still at large, and he told me that all along the Syrian coast, as well as inland, the presence of plague had been suspected for two months past; but they had received scant news thence, and hoped the disease had not spread. As I had to touch at these ports this was another unpleasantness for me, but still I resolved to go back on board, and with the first fair wind to leave Cyprus, in hope of finding better luck in Syria. I bid the Tuscan consul farewell, and embarked that evening.

Cyprus had been free from plague for 30 years, and now it was brought by some sailors saved from the wreck of a Turkish xebec from Alexandria, which foundered off Paphos. Nicosia, whither the survivors had gone for refuge, was first attacked. I learned later that the disease had spread over the whole island, and did not cease until June of that year, 1760, after the deaths of 22,000 persons.

On February 8 I left the roadstead of Salines, and the next day arrived at Caifa in Syria, the season not allowing us to anchor at Acre, a port eight miles to the north.

CHAPTER XXVI.

SUNDRY NOTES ON CYPRUS.

(Viaggio, 1787. T. II. Cap. IX.)

§ I.   *The divisions of the island in old time, and under
the present government.*

It is well known that Cyprus once comprised nine kingdoms,
or rather that its soil was divided between nine petty princes,
each of whom had his own capital and court. These were
[in the 4th cent. B.C. Salamis, Citium, with Idalium and
Tamassus, Marium, Amathus, Curium, Paphos, Soloi, Lapethos,
Ceryneia. *Diodorus*, XVI. 42.]
The island was then divided into four Provinces, viz.
Salamina, Amathusia, Paphia, and Lapethia. We should
perhaps understand that the Kings of Salamis, Amathus,
Paphos (old or new) and Lapethos possessed a larger territory
than the other five, or enjoyed some kind of precedence among
them. The fourfold division appears to have prevailed under
the rule of the Egyptians and Romans.
Under the Lusignan dynasty there were 12 districts:
Nicosia, Famagusta, Limasol, Pafo, Cerines, Saline, Mes-
sarea, Carpasso, Mazoto, Afdimu, Chrusochou, Pentaia. After
the Turkish conquest these became seven *Sanjaqs*, whose
names I do not know. But this distribution fell gradually

into disuse, and the Turks themselves have adopted the arrangement most convenient to the Christian inhabitants. For as the population dwindled, and the prosperity of the island decayed, it was re-divided into four districts, corresponding with the sees of the four Greek bishops. Salamina, on the east, including Carpas and the Mesarian plain, was annexed to the archbishopric of Nicosia, Cerines, on the north, including the lands of Chrysochou and Pendaia, to the bishopric of Kyrenia. Paphos, on the west, including Soloi, to the see of Paphos: and Citium, including the district of Limasol and Salines on the south, to the see of Citium, whose bishop now resides in Larnaca.

§ II. *The Dragoman of the Serai.*

The Dragoman of the Serai holds one of the principal posts assigned to a Christian. His title signifies "interpreter in the Governor's palace," but he is really the agent who treats between the Christian population and the Governor. I was wrong in saying he held a *firman* from the Porte. He is nominated directly by the bishops, who are ready to change him if he is not acceptable to the government. He must be a man of sense and tact, for his position is a very important one.

The bishops agree to pay him four *paras* on each item of the poll tax or *kharaj*: and he represents them in all dealings with the Governor, not in their spiritual capacity as bishops, but as the natural leaders of the people. As such they bind themselves to pay to the *Muhassil*, through the dragoman, a fixed poll tax, reckoned according to the population. Besides this, the inhabitants of their own free will pay 50 purses, or 25,000 piastres, to anticipate and prevent the exactions which capriciously, without reason or form of law, but suggested simply by calumnious tyranny, might fall upon them. But the Governor may accept these terms or not, as he pleases.

They are arranged between the *Muhassil* and the dragoman, and this point settled the former has no right to levy any further contributions, beyond the duty on food stuffs exported. But he gets 20,000 piastres from anyone invested with the rank of *Agha*, and 1000 piastres from each bishop as the contribution of his calogeroi or monks. He exacts other dues upon produce, and taxes the people to reimburse his expenditure both public and personal. The bishops, through the dragoman, agree to these impositions, which make the post of *Muhassil* very lucrative: if the holder is not a person of the highest honesty his gains are immense.

I do not know of any other country peopled by Greeks under Turkish rule where the bishops are the representatives of the people. When Cyprus was taken from the Venetians the Greek inhabitants found themselves without leaders of position, education or experience, their best men having fallen in defence of their country, and so were constrained to put forward their bishops.

§ III.   *Population.*

It is an extremely difficult thing to avoid error in calculating the population of any city or province in the Turkish Empire. The farther the locality lies from the capital, the more difficult the task, in the islands it is almost impossible. The safest basis is the list of persons subject to *kharaj* or poll tax, generally reckoned as a third of the whole population. But these lists are affected by the particular agreements made, arbitrarily enough, between the government and the bishops. In Cyprus especially, where the bishops act as agents of the Christian community, the interest of individuals can easily override the public interest, and so an exact estimate of the population of the island is almost impossible.

After very careful search I had determined that the number of Cypriots assessed for *kharaj* was 12,000. Add the two-thirds who are ordinarily exempt, you have 36,000. Still I neither believed the estimate to be correct nor the number of inhabitants to be so small, so I set it down as 40,000. But a letter from Signor Stefano Saraf, an old inhabitant of Cyprus, dated September 2, 1771, showed me that I had omitted to include the Turks. Further information in his possession, derived from the assessment of *kharaj* made in 1767, led him to put the total population at 120,000.

§ IV.   *The Year of the Venetian Occupation.*

The Venetians succeeded to the administration of the island from 1475, after the death of King Jacques III, son of Caterina Cornaro. The republic then aspired to absolute rule, and proposed to the Queen that she should retire to Venice with the royal title, resigning the administration into their hands. She had no great inclination so to do, but as the Venetians had already command of the troops and the fortresses at last she gave her consent. The eloquent persuasiveness of her brother George Cornaro, who had been specially sent from Venice, and arrived in Cyprus January 24, 1489, greatly influenced her decision. He was followed by General Francesco Priuli, who anchored his fleet at Famagusta February 21, 1489. The matter then was quickly arranged. On February 15th Caterina came from Nicosia to Famagusta, and on the 26th, after celebration of the Mass of the Holy Spirit, resigned the kingdom into the hands of General Priuli, consigning to him at the same time the standard of the republic, which was immediately hoisted in the square of Famagusta. Two days later, February 28, 1489, the cession was formally completed: the Commissioners of the republic swore that the kingdom should be still governed according to the *Assise* or Laws of Jerusalem, and the nobles of Cyprus swore allegiance to the republic, in the presence of the Commissioners. The standard of St Mark was then hoisted on the fortress of Famagusta.

The memory of the event is preserved in an inscription engraved on a stone in the wall behind the altar of the Cathedral Church of Famagusta. Although this became a mosque the stone remained there until the year 1736, when the building was injured by an earthquake. In the restoration the stone was removed, but may still be seen on the ground in a room near the choir, which is now disused, but contains many other bits of marble, heaped pell mell, fragments of tombstones which formerly lay on the floor of the church. Here is the inscription. Note that the year is given in the old style, 1488.

FRANCISCO DE PRIOLIS VENETAE CLASSI
IMPERANTE DIVI MARCI VEXILLUM
CYPRI FELICITER ERECTUM EST

AN. MCCCCLXXXVIII. XXVIII. FEBRVAR.

Francesco de' Priuli being in command of the Venetian fleet, the standard of St Mark was happily raised in Cyprus, February 28, 1488.

Queen Catharine left Cyprus on May 14, and after a prosperous voyage reached Venice May 31. She was conducted to St Mark's, and there confirmed her resignation of the kingdom. The ratification of her act was sent to Cyprus, where on July 20, 1489, the banner of St Mark was hoisted in all the fortresses, cities and villages of the island. From this date is reckoned the establishment of the sovereignty of Venice in Cyprus.

§ V. *The Grand Dukes of Tuscany of the family of Medici attempt to acquire the island.*

At the time when the Grand Duke Ferdinand I turned his attention to Syria, to establish an advantageous intercourse with the celebrated Fakr-ed-din, Emir of the Druses, his mind always full of great schemes, conceived the idea of the conquest of Cyprus. This is noted in the History of the Grand Duchy of Tuscany by the well-known Secretary Abate Galluzzi. The first attack was to be made upon the fortress of Famagusta, which was to be taken by surprise under a secret understanding with 6000 Greeks, who had promised to rise, and to assist in the surrender.

To this effect a fleet left Leghorn in 1607 composed of eight galleys, and nine other vessels, galleons and *bertoni*, and 2200 soldiers under the Marquis Francesco del Monte, who had the command of this fleet which was unluckily scattered at sea, and arrived before Famagusta in a less effective condition than the occasion required. However they made the attempt, but not finding the support promised them by the Greeks, the fleet retired, not without loss.

The untoward end of this expedition was attributed to the disaster at sea, and to the perfidy of the Greeks. In the Diary of Settimanni, a MS. in the Magliabechian Library in Florence, it is asserted that the Grand Duke was badly served by his commander: an opinion from which I am not prepared to differ, because in the following year, 1608, was composed by Captain Jacques Pierre a memorandum on the attack on Famagusta, preserved in the Archives of the Old Secretariat of His Royal Highness, from various passages of which I gather that the plan failed through sundry shortcomings in the commander. The said Captain Jacques Pierre drew up this paper at the request of Ferdinand I who, great Prince that he was, would not forego this enterprise at a time when the relative strength of his naval forces and those of the Turks made him almost sure of success.

The Grand Duke proposed to employ two galleons and six galleys which were already at sea under the orders of the Chevalier de Beauregard, a Frenchman but sprung from the house of Guadagni, of Florence. On the other hand, Jacques Pierre, considering that these vessels had been a long time at sea, that their hulls wanted repairs and their crews rest, thought that in their stead they should use four other large vessels and four *patacce*, with which he was sure that they might undertake some enterprise in the Levant, and even if the attempt on Famagusta failed they might attack the *Caravan*. This *Caravan* was the squadron of Turkish ships which sailed yearly from Alexandria to Constantinople after the return of the pilgrims from Mecca. I may mention that on October 20, 1608, this very squadron under M. de Beauregard successfully attacked these ships, the Grand Duke himself allowing that the prize money reached 2,000,000 ducats, without counting the ransoms paid for many Turks of distinction who were taken prisoners.

Jacques Pierre's report goes on to say that he does not think the summer season best suited for the attempt on Famagusta, because the seas are then full of vessels, and the destination of the Tuscan fleet would be easier to discover. The long winter nights are more suitable. He thinks 1700 soldiers and 800 stout sailors sufficient. He knows every corner of the city, and believes it would be easily taken. He was going on to say what action the fleet should take on arrival, but breaks off his report, as the death of Ferdinand I on February 6, 1690, caused the abandonment of the enterprise.

But the conquest of Cyprus always remained within the view of the Medicean princes, for I have read in the same Old Secretariat a proposal made by a Cypriot, Maximilian Tronchi, to the Grand Duke Ferdinand II when he visited

Venice in 1628. This paper contains various notices of the condition of the island at that date. There were only four fortresses, Paphos, Limasol, Cerines and Salines, and two cities, Nicosia and Famagusta. In each fortress were 100 horsemen and 100 foot soldiers. In Nicosia 400 horse and 400 infantry: in Famagusta 200 horse and 200 infantry. In the rest of the island there might be among Turks and renegades 8000 men, while there were 10,000 Christians ready to take up arms against their masters.

The writer proposes to make a feigned attack on Paphos, Limasol and Cerines, to divide the troops in the island; then to land in force at Salines, and to march with 6000 or 7000 infantry to Nicosia, while the naval forces attacked Famagusta by sea and land. Victory would be certain, for he remembers that when the fleet of Ferdinand I approached, although all the janissaries, cavalry and infantry, were under arms they had so great fear of defeat, that they had determined it would be wiser to surrender at the very moment when the Tuscan fleet on leaving the harbour fired its last three shots at the fortress. He notes next the artillery then in Famagusta. Five cannons only were serviceable, the rest being dismounted and without carriages. The enterprise would require 10,000 men, 20 vessels and six galleys, with other preparations and provisions on a grand scale. Arms were especially required to supply to the Christian islanders who would take their side. There was nothing extravagant in this, since Tronchi was planning the general conquest of the island. But it would have been wiser first to secure possession of Famagusta, for with the fall of this fortress the conquest of Cyprus might be deemed assured.

This plan too fell to the ground; and the jealous aims of no other Power have been directed at Cyprus, which remains in the hands of the Turks.

CHAPTER XXVII.

NOTES ON THE TURKISH MOSQUE IN CYPRUS CALLED TEKYE.

NEAR the salt lake at Larnaca is a Mosque called the Teke, which I saw for the first time in 1761. Since that date the reverence paid to it, and the buildings themselves have been steadily increasing, and on my return to the island I paid it another visit, and here append a few notes on a shrine which is acquiring a certain importance among the Turks.

The word *Teke*, better written *Tekye*, is derived from the Turkish *Tek*, meaning *quiet, alone*, and bears the same meaning as our monastery, from the Greek μόνος.

The building stands on the west shore of the salt lake; within it is a tomb, which was for some time considered to contain the remains of Mohammad's mother. The dervishes now teach that the tomb is that of his aunt; but they know not her name or lineage, and both ascriptions are equally false. The Moslem call her *Umm haram, bint Milhan*, "Revered mother, daughter of Milhan," but this is a title rather than a name. Many suppose that she came to Cyprus when the Saracens conquered the island, and died here, but they bring no proof or evidence of their belief. What is known of the origin of the shrine I will here set down.

In the early years of the eighteenth century a dervish of a speculative turn discovered and dug out a common-place Moslem tomb, and thought it might be a profitable business to inspire the shepherds who fed their flocks thereabouts with a veneration for the place. Old Cypriot Christians assert that it was he who, in furtherance of this project, circulated the story of miracles performed at the tomb.

Mohammadans however hold that the tomb was under ground, and being exposed by rains was found by some shepherds, to whom on entering it there appeared a lady of beautiful and majestic aspect, clothed in white and shining garments. They were astounded, but their fears were soon stilled by the lady who blessed them and their flocks, and revealed to them that she was the aunt of Mohammad, and that her body lay in the tomb which they had found. The vision, which they believed sent by their prophet, who wished to point out for their veneration his aunt's sepulchre, filled them with comfort and happiness, and thenceforth their flocks were ever more and more fruitful. The dervish no doubt had accomplices, who spread through the island the news of the discovery. Crowds rushed to the place: the sick were healed, the lame walked, and left for their homes in perfect health. Such virtue, it was said, lay in the mere touch of the stones.

Offerings rolled in, and the dervish had wherewith to adorn the shrine he had created. His efforts, and the influence of certain devotees, procured him leave from the government to build over the tomb a suitable dome, under which a few persons could assemble, as is customary throughout the East, at the tomb of any notable saint.

Time passed, and the shrine, though frequented and honoured by devotees in the island, was little known beyond it. When the plague of 1760 had ceased, the *Muhassil,* Mehmed Agha, made a kind of wooden barrier to enclose and guard the tomb. But in Islam men are not allowed to congregate with women, so an Imam was appointed to direct the devotions of men, while his wife attended the women. Ajem Ali Agha, the successor of Mehmed Agha, removed in 1761 the wooden barrier, and enclosed the shrine with a wall, closed by two gates of bronze, adorned with foliage worked in low relief, one at each end of the tomb. By these women can enter to pay their devotions at the shrine, and at such times men may not penetrate beyond the outer wall.

Representations were made to the Sultan of the origin, the miracles and the sanctity of the tomb, and permission was readily granted to build a Mosque, and to do all that was possible to increase the dignity and sanctity of the spot. The work was completed with such grandeur and solidity as was possible in a place where the arts were so little studied, and was crowned with three domes, the largest in the middle covered the tomb. Two tall *minarés* or *campanili* were built close by, upon which the *muezzins*, officials like the Roman *praecones*, stand to announce to the faithful the hours of prayer. Dwelling rooms were also added for the convenience of devotees and pilgrims, and for the dervishes who have charge of the shrine. A running stream too was brought to the place, and a fountain with eight jets serves the Moslem with water, to which they ascribe sanctifying properties, for their ablutions.

The fame of the sanctuary thus enlarged and adorned spread throughout the Ottoman Empire, and to give it still greater dignity the Sultan conferred on it his special protection, and sent a sheikh who should hold for life the office of guardian. From that time forth it has become a regular place of pilgrimage, and from every quarter Moslem bring offerings of money, silver lamps, carpets and other ornaments suitable to their worship. Lands have been assigned to it, whose revenues contribute to its further adornment, as well as to the maintenance of the dervishes who have it in their charge.

The example is instructive. A Moslem creates an object of veneration and worship out of a humble unknown tomb, built up of four stones without inscription or any particular marks of distinction. He has been deceived, but is satisfied, for what are all the mysteries of his faith but so many deceits.

A certain Greek writer Constantinos (Porphyrogennetos, περὶ θεμάτων, χν.) says that Abubekr was the first Moslem who crossed over to Cyprus and made himself master of it in the reign of Heraclius, adding that his daughter died there, and that the place of her burial is still shown. In order to admit that this Tekye arose thus, and that the tomb is really that of the daughter of Abubekr, we have to face many difficulties. But we have Sheikh el Maqin and Abu'l Feda, both among the most trustworthy of Arabic writers, who tell us that the first Arab invasion of Cyprus was led by Moawiyeh (under the khalifate of Othman) who arrived with a large fleet in A.H. 27 (A.D. 647). They would have hardly made so great an error, or have failed to tell us if Abubekr, the first Khalife, had attempted the conquest of Cyprus before Moawiyeh. But even granted that this were so, and that the daughter of Abubekr died and was buried here, the Moslem would have called her the kinswoman, not the aunt of Mohammad, for Abubekr was his father-in-law. In short, as their own tradition is but vague, and the history of their khalifate gives it no support, we may conclude that the untrustworthy story of Constantinos formed the framework of the legend which has grown round this shrine, whose fame is still daily on the increase.

[See "The Story of Umm Harám" in Turkish and English. *Journal of the Royal Asiatic Society*, January, 1897. Mariti (p. 184) forgets that C. Van Bruyn saw the tomb, and knew its attribution, in 1683. *Excerpta Cypria*, 240.]

CHAPTER XXVIII.

ON THE ASP OF CYPRUS.

I GLADLY adjoin here a description of the asp of Cyprus with which I am favoured by a friend who has resided in the island for 20 years. He informs me that what I wrote concerning the κουφή or deaf snake is applicable rather to another snake called κεράστης or horned, equally venomous, but not always mortal.

"The asp of Cyprus (*vipera mauritanica*) is a snake from three to five feet long, and from four to fifteen inches round, according to its age and the soil on which it is found. Its poison is deadly, but less acid and active than that of the Egyptian asp. The person bitten is tortured for 18 or 20 hours, and death is preceded by pallor, inflammation and convulsions.

The head is small in proportion to the body, and somewhat flat; the mouth very large, ending only where the neck begins. The muzzle round, nostrils broad, eyes small and dark under a projecting brow. The neck thin, but growing in bulk until it joins the belly. The tail ends in a thick fleshy point, on which is a short hard sharp spine. The skin of the back is an ashen or leaden grey, scaly and bright. It is dotted with darker spots: near and on the belly the spots may be white, or white and grey.

It is called κουφὴ or deaf, the country folk believing it is
six months deaf and six months blind. The men who catch
them say they use some charm, and further assert that when
the creature is blind its eyes are smeared with some viscous
humour, which makes them swell and close. This is all fable.
I have seen many asps, but all had their sight. The ancients,
David among them, believed it to be deaf. 'Their poison
is like the poison of a serpent; they are like the deaf adder
that stoppeth her ear: which hearkeneth not to the voice of
charmers, charming never so wisely,' Ps. lviii. 4, 5, and it
ought at least to be deaf, for it has no ears. I observed this
fact on an asp four feet long; yet I would not say that nature
has thus distinguished it from other animals, for the conduit
which conveys sound to its sensorium may communicate with
the aesophagus or the nostrils, or with that tiny tube through
which it hisses. But this would be hard to see, and therefore
to prove.

Its mouth, as I said, is very large, and can be stretched so
as to swallow quite large animals. I have seen quails and
partridges in them, and others have found hares. Its jaws
have two rows of bones, the outer near the lips, the inner
on the palate. The outer jaw is covered with fleshy ex-
crescences, like bladders but of strong stout skin, under which
on each side is a double fang, long curved, very sharp and
piercing: it has the appearance of two teeth joined together, is
very white and hard. It is not fixed, but bends inwards: when
the snake wants to bite it erects the fang, which pierces the
vesicle round it, then it strikes and pressing in the fang stirs in
the wound the poison exuded from the vesicle. The lower
jaw has one bone only, armed on each side with five small
sharp teeth almost buried in the skin. In the upper jaw the
inner bone is shaped into a kind of point, and has on each
side six small sharp hard and pointed teeth transparently white,
like fishes' scales, set sloping towards the throat, and like the
upper row buried in thick skin. The lower jawbone is not

continuous, but an interval in front allows a tube to be seen
through which the snake can emit a strong strident hiss.
Through this too issues its tongue, of a dark reddish brown,
ending in two sharp points like the sting of a large wasp.
This it can vibrate with very great speed, and so stirs up the
active properties of its poison, which grows more pungent and
subtle.

This poison is a yellowish fluid, acid and volatile, held
in the vesicles which cover its two chief fangs. These are
always immersed in the fluid, which as they strike they mix
with the blood. Their bite is so quick and light as to be
hardly felt, but the part begins at once to swell, the man grows
pale, and then livid, as the poison clogs the veins. In a few
hours he is seized with a deadly lethargy, accompanied by
nausea and depression: then a general sense of oppression,
followed by tremors and convulsions. The circulation gets
gradually feebler, and at last the blood is wholly congealed,
and the man dies.

This terrible reptile is generally killed by a tiny insect.
The snake lives among stones, shady rocks and in damp soil;
here it is attacked, usually on the back, by a very small red
ant, which pierces the skin, burrows through its vitals and
destroys it.

Cypriots believe that the herb called sow-thistle (*cicerbita*
or *sonchus oleraceus*) can neutralise the asp's bite. Several
villagers of Kythrea saw a toad come out of a stream and
proceed to feed on an asp which lay dead on the bank. From
time to time it went to eat of a plant which grew hard by.
The men rooted up the plant to watch how its loss would affect
the toad. This animal, after eating again of the asp, sought
its usual antidote, and when it could not find it grew wild and
troubled, at last a kind of convulsion threw it on its back, and
in a few minutes it was dead. This does not of course prove
that the sow-thistle is a complete antidote to the bite of the
asp, but it leads us to believe that the skin and flesh of the

reptile contain acrid elements which contaminate the blood, and that the said herb can mitigate their effect." So far my friend.

Cyprus always abounded in serpents, whence among its many names it got that of Ophiusa. In the village of Tremithus there is a family believed to be endowed with the gift or virtue of curing persons bitten by snakes. Étienne de Lusignan in his *Chorograffia* (Bologna, 1573, p. 22 a) says that in his day men were found who caught all kinds of snakes, and were bitten by them without feeling any harm. They believe themselves to be the descendants of the ancient Ophiogenes, a Cypriot family, who held the wound of a person who had been bitten to their lips, and by sucking it healed him. Nor had the snakes any power against them. When the Romans held the island, in wonderment at this power they sent Exagon, a member of the family, to Rome, where people saw and marvelled at the truth of what they had heard. Pliny, XXVIII. 3, writes "In certain men the whole body is endowed with a charm : thus members of those families which are a terror to serpents heal persons bitten by a mere touch, or slight suction. Of this kind are the Psylli and Marsi, and those who in Cyprus are called Ophiogenes. One of this race, Exagon by name, was sent to Rome, and by order of the consuls, to try his power, thrown into a cask full of snakes, which, to the wonder of all, fondled about him." (Cf. Cyprianos, *History of Cyprus*, 4to., Venice, 1788, pp. 398—400).

CHAPTER XXIX.

OF THE SITE OF CITIUM.

(Dissertazione istorico-critica sull' antica Città di Citium.
Livorno, 1787.)

A FRIEND of mine, who passed some years in Cyprus, writes from Aix in Provence to challenge my opinion expressed in Chap. III. that in the town of Larnaca, and not in the village of Citi, is to be sought the site of the ancient city of Citium. I must see if I cannot strengthen and add to the arguments which already appear to me conclusive.

I am inclined to believe that Citium, certainly one of the oldest cities in the world, was the first point of the island to be inhabited. We read in Genesis x. 4, 5 "the sons of Javan; Elishah, and Tarshish, Kittim, and Dodanim. Of these were the isles of the nations divided in their lands, every one after his tongue; after their families, in their nations." Kittim was probably the one who first reached Cyprus, and from him it took its name Cetima or Chetima. For the derivation of the Greek form Cition we have the testimony of Josephus, *Ant.* I. II. "Now Chetimos possessed the island Chetima. This is now called Cypros, and from it all the islands and most of the seaside places were called by the Hebrews Chetim. I call as a witness one of the cities in Cypros, which has succeeded in preserving the name. For it is called by those who gave it a Greek form Cition, which does not depart very widely from Chetimus."

We need not insist that Kittim was the builder of Citium. He may have been the first to settle inhabitants there, who were reinforced later by Phoenician colonists. Indeed the foundation of Citium, as well as of Lapethos, is ascribed to Belus, King of Tyre.

Of the vicissitudes of Citium, and its famous men, I have spoken briefly in Chap. III. The nine kingdoms of Cyprus fell under the successors of Alexander, but the final destruction of Citium I would put as late as A.D. 210.

Now where was the city situate? Ptolemy and Strabo set it west of Cape Dades, which I identify with Cape Pyla, my friend with Cape Citi. It is true that Cape Citi is thus left without an ancient name. But Porcacchi, Lusignan and later travellers were misled by the similarity of the names into fixing the site of ancient Citium upon that of the modern village of Citi, whereas it really occupied a part of the present town of Larnaca, stretching thence towards the newer suburb of Salines. Of its port, the same which Strabo calls "a closed harbour," the remains were in my day fully visible, and on a hill above it a windmill occupied the room of some old light-tower or fort. In Citi no vestige has been found of ancient buildings; whereas in Larnaca, besides the great squared stones which are daily dug out to serve for modern houses, even up to 1783 Roman inscriptions, and other relics of antiquity were often brought to light. Again, the great salt lake of which Pliny speaks (XXXI. 74, 84) lies nearer to Larnaca than to Citi.

Diodorus Siculus sets the distance from Salamis to Citium at 200 stadia or 25 miles. This is perhaps somewhat under the truth; but if Citium were at Citi we should have to add 48 stadia more, making the whole distance nearer 300 than 200 stadia.

We are agreed as to the derivation of Larnaca from the

Greek *larnax*, a coffin or tomb. But I cannot therefore accept the suggestion that Larnaca was the necropolis of a village more than six miles distant.

Besides the sarcophagi found in 1766 by Signor Zambelli's masons, my friend mentions a remarkable tomb found under the house of one Ianni, a Cypriot watchmaker, consisting of a large vaulted chamber supported by two arches, and containing two sarcophagi with bones indicating a stature beyond that of the tallest men of our days. Also in the garden of the house known as that of "the three cypresses," then inhabited by a French merchant, M. Hermitte, were laid open four sepulchral chambers of different sizes, constructed on the same model. Similar remains are noted by Dapper.

The first settlers, be they who they may, certainly sought out the most convenient landing-place; and their successors, always a seafaring and trading folk, would certainly have used and improved the facilities open to them at Larnaca, which are altogether wanting at Citi.

Shall I convince my good friend? I hope so; but I remember Martial's wise saying

> " Aurum et opes, et rura frequens donabit amicus.
> Qui velit ingenio cedere rarus erit,"

and leave an impartial public to decide between us.

THE SIEGES OF
NICOSIA AND FAMAGUSTA

BY

GIO. PIETRO CONTARINI

AND

COUNT NESTOR MARTINENGO

1572

PREFATORY NOTE

THE deep interest felt by Christian Europe in the fateful
sieges of Nicosia and Famagusta is seen in the ample material
at the command of the later historian. On them indeed
hang the next 300 years of Cypriot history. It is fortunate
for us that men who had lived through them were willing
to recall and record such appalling scenes, to describe how
they had escaped death, and endured slavery. Contemporary
accounts are neither few nor meagre. I doubt if the sieges
of Delhi and Lucknow have had more, or more spirited,
chroniclers.

I will notice here what is already in print: other personal
narratives may lie unnoticed in manuscript in Italian libraries.
One, perhaps the most valuable, the *Narration* of Angelo
Gatto, was published as late as 1895, and the new edition
of my *Excerpta Cypria* gives a translation of another by
F. Falchetti, from a MS. still unprinted at Pesaro. Benedetti,
Membre, and one or two other pamphlets which I have not
been able to see, are noted in my *Bibliography of Cyprus*,
under dates 1570—73.

The official or general historians are of course to be consulted. Diedo, Paruta (see *Excerpta Cypria*, pp. 87—119),
Conti, Manolesso, Guarnerius, Knolles, Foglietta, Graziani
(of the last two I have printed translations), de Thou, Jauna,
Arrighi, Romanin, have all chapters on the War of Cyprus.

It is not a little remarkable that not one of these writers
even mentions the many striking buildings, ecclesiastical or
civil, other than the fortifications, which adorned Nicosia and
Famagusta. The havoc and desolation, especially in the latter
city, which we see and lament to-day, must date from the
sieges, yet none of those who defended the walls thought of
describing for us how the cities looked from within.

> "Others to a city strong
> Lay siege, encamped; by battery, scale and mine
> Assaulting: others from the wall defend
> With dart and javelin, stones, and sulphurous fire;
> On each hand slaughter and gigantic deeds."

GIO. PIETRO CONTARINI wrote a general history of the whole war, from the first move made by Sultan Selim to the Turkish defeat off Lepanto, October 7, 1572, which was printed at Venice in that year. He does not mention his authorities, but gives a connected account of the movements of the fleet and armies of both Turks and Christians, including naturally episodes, such as were the sieges of Nicosia and Famagusta. He gives very fully the numbers and disposition of the opposing forces, with the names of the officers, and exact dates.

COUNT NESTOR MARTINENGO, an officer who came to Famagusta in the train of Hieronimo Martinengo (who died on the voyage), succeeded during the siege to the command of a company, was twice wounded, enslaved at the fall of the city, escaped thence, and returned to Venice to make his report to the Doge. This *Relatione di tutto il Successo di Famagosta*, a little pamphlet of 16 pages ($5\frac{7}{8} \times 4$ in.), bears the imprint "Venetia, Appresso Giorgio Angelieri, MD. LXXII." Within a year it was translated into English, French and German; and borrowed almost verbatim, but without acknowledgment, by Calepio, Bizarri, Sereno, Foglietta and Graziani. As the *Report of all the Successes of Famagosta* it was "Englished out of Italian" by William Malim, and "Imprinted at London by John Daye, an. 1572."

Malim's version, a rare volume ($7\frac{1}{4} \times 5\frac{1}{8}$ in.) comprises, besides (5) "The true Report &c.," pp. 24—77, (1) a title and epistle dedicatory to the Earl of Leicester, Baron of Denbigh,

K.G., dated March 23, 1572, 15 pp., pedantic and fulsome. Malim was at Constantinople in 1564, had visited Cyprus, and met at Paphos the Governor, Lorenzo Tiepolo ; also at Corfu Gio. Ant. Querini (the first of these was hanged, the latter beheaded, on the surrender), (2) "a briefe description of the Iland of Cyprus," pp. 16—19, (3) an address "to the Reader," wherein he speaks of "being precisely tyed to mine author's meaning," (4) 26 Latin elegiacs, "in Turchas precatio." The translation itself is quaint and diffuse, but correct. The present version is new. The opening and closing paragraphs, marked by brackets, are restored from MS. 117 of the Biblioteca Oliveriana at Pesaro.

ANGELO CALEPIO, a Dominican monk, and Vicar General of the Order in Cyprus, was present throughout the siege and sack of Nicosia. His mother Lucretia was slain on the taking of the city—"they cut off her head on her serving-maid's lap." He was captured by a Dervish, sold with his two sisters to the captain of a galley, ransomed for 4500 aspers : again imprisoned at Constantinople as a papal spy, again released, and restored unhurt to a convent of his Order at Bologna. He contributed an account of both sieges to the *Chorograffia* of Fra. S. de Lusignan, published in Italian at Bologna in 1572, and in French at Paris, 1580. (*Excerpta Cypria*, p. 122.)

FABRIANO FALCHETTI, a soldier from a village near Rimini, tells briefly what he saw and suffered, until, when the city surrendered, he was made a prisoner, sold for 16 sequins to a renegade, and lay for 20 days chained on a galley. (*Excerpta Cypria*, p. 80.)

ANGELO GATTO, of Orvieto, wrote a *Narrazione* which was published by a priest of his birthplace in 1895. It is compiled *soldatescamente*, in style "rude and unpolished, but quite true and natural." It was addressed "from the Tower of the Black Sea" to Adriano (brother of Astorre) Baglione, and dated November 19, 1573. It is the most detailed and the longest of all the accounts, occupying 100 pages 4to, and the fullest in names and dates. It is in fact almost a diary of the siege.

Gatto was serving at Famagusta as Ensign to Capt. Carlo Ragonasco : on July 5 he got his company, on July 30 he was wounded by a musket-ball in the shoulder. Special information is due to him on (1) the coining of the well-known siege-pieces inscribed "Pro regni Cypri præsidio, Venetorum fides inviolabilis," "bisanti di ramo da diece soldi l'uno, e soldi da quattro quattrini": (2) the composition and use of Greek fire (cf. T. A. Archer, *The Crusade of Richard I,* p. 72): (3) the victualling of the garrison: (4) the journey to Constantinople, and the inhuman treatment of the captives. The voyage took from Sept. 22 to Nov. 2; their imprisonment was rigorous, their treatment cruel until May 1572, when the efforts of Giacomo Malatesta, Marchese di Ronco-Freddo, procured some alleviation of their condition. But we hear nothing of the writer's release or subsequent fate.

The "LAMENT OF CYPRUS." We are greatly indebted to M. Simos Menardos for the publication (Athens, 1906) under the title Θρῆνος τῆς Κύπρου, of a MS. discovered in 1903 at Phasoulla in the district of Limasol. It contained 777 Saturnian verses (στίχοι πολιτικοὶ, rhyming lines of 15 syllables), the work of a contemporary ποιητάρις, who describes the siege and fall of Nicosia, and the opening scenes of the siege of Famagusta. It is a rude production, of more glossological than historical value, but the writer saw what he described, and lost two children, whom the Turks took as slaves. And it is the only account we have from the hand of an Orthodox native.

It mentions among the churches of the capital turned into mosques the royal church of Hagia Sophia; Hagia Caterina, ὁποῦταν πισκοπᾶτον; the Eleousa, near the last; and the Hodegetria, ὁποῦν καθολικᾶτον.

The calling of a στιχουργὸς or ποιητάρις exists still, and is still, as M. Menardos says, an ἐπάγγελμα βιοποριστικὸν; its simple rules being learned from older hands, and put to use when a murder, the death of a bishop, an escape from prison, or any like startling event stirs the bard, and loosens the purse-strings of his patrons. It would not be fair to compare these stilted narratives, hampered by their cumbrous form, with the *rispetti, stornelli, strambotti* which an Italian of the same class trolls out with real passion and easy grace. In one is seen job-work, in the other the "inexhaustible affluence" of improvisation.

ALESSANDRO PODACATORO left Nicosia before the siege of that city for Famagusta, with a brother, who was killed on the ravelin, and made a report to Melchiorre Michiel (ob. 1572), who had been in 1558 Governor of Cyprus. He raised in his own villages, clothed and drilled, a company of 300 native soldiers, with whom he served during the siege. He was taken prisoner, chained for 37 days on a galley, and ransomed by the French consul for 325 sequins. He heard from the mouth of the Genoese renegade who flayed Bragadino the details of his cruel death. The narrative wears a genuine look, and gives many interesting details not found elsewhere. Two of the writer's kin, Livio, who was succeeded in 1553 by his brother Cesare, were titular archbishops of Nicosia. Two more were in 1547 and 1552 abbots of the monastery of Santa Croce. Louis and Hector were slain at Nicosia, another Livio was enslaved. His *Relazione* was printed at Venice, 1876.

From the pen of ANTONIO RICCOBONI, of Rovigo, we have an account, in neat Latin, of the same siege. No authorities are quoted, and letters and speeches set out in full give it the air of an academic exercise: but the writer, a Professor at Padua, 1571—99, was a contemporary of the events he relates. It was first printed at Venice in 1843.

BARTOLOMEO SERENO was a Roman of good family, born about 1520; fought in the army of Charles IX against the Huguenots at Moncontour, and on the galleys of Pius V against the Turks at Lepanto. He took the Benedictine habit in the abbey of Monte Cassino in 1576, and died there about 1604. His *Commentari della Guerra di Cipro* were first published in 1845 by the monks of Monte Cassino from an autograph in their famous library as the first volume of the *Archivio Cassinese*. (See pp. 8—10, 53—65, 238—252.)

GIO. SOZOMENO addressed a report, printed at Bologna in 1571, to the Grand Duke of Tuscany. He was a Cypriot, an engineer, who possessed the science which allowed him to form a clear judgment on what went on around him, and the courage to express it. He too was made a prisoner at Nicosia, after seeing his elder daughter burnt to death, and leaving another in the hands of the Turks. (*Excerpta Cypria*, pp. 81—87.)

BERNARDINO TOMITANO, professor of logic at Padua, went to Cyprus as the friend and physician of Astorre Baglione, wrote an account of both sieges, and returned to die at Venice in 1576. The story of Nicosia was printed at Padua, 1846, and a fragment containing the surrender of Famagusta at Venice, 1858. They seem extracted from a life of Astorre Baglione.

PLANS.

(1) cm. 22 × 17. NICOSSIA (a pair with Famagosta (1) ?), river turned into the fosse N. and S.

(1) cm. 22 × 16·5. Inscribed FAMAGOSTA.

(2) cm. 27 × 18. In Bressa, 1571, dedicated to Signor Cap. Negrobon by Stephano Gibellino.

(3) cm. 36 × 26. Il vero ritratto della citta di Famagosta et fortezza &c. il anno 1571. 𝕵𝕮

(4) cm. 19·5 × 11. " Famagosta, 42."

GIO. PIETRO CONTARINI. Historia delle cose successe dal principio della guerra mossa da Selim Ottomano a' Venetiani fino al dì della gran Giornata vittoriosa contra Turchi (pp. 9—13). 4to. Venice, 1572.

THE SIEGE OF NICOSIA.

ON July 1, 1570, Piali and his fleet reached Limissò in the island of Cyprus, where they landed at once, and made many of the inhabitants slaves. The following day Piali, with all the galleys and other vessels, went to the Salines, where they met with no resistance, to the great delight of all: and on the 3rd at their convenience, and without any hindrance, all the infantry, cavalry, artillery, with all their equipment, were landed. No opposition was offered by the troops on shore, for these thought it best so, considering that with the small force of cavalry at their command they could not prevent a landing; for the circuit of the island was 600 miles, and the distance from the Salines to Nicosia 30—if it had been only four or six they would have made the attempt. So the *Stradiot* horse which was with the Count of Roccas at the Salines retired to Nicosia. Mustafa, who had made himself master of the country round, after causing certain repairs to be executed at the Salines, sent Piali with 100 galleys, 20 horseboats, and 12 lighters to the gulf of Aiazzo to take on board more horses, *Sipahi* and Janissaries, and at the same time despatched Ali with the rest of the fleet to the gulf of Settelia to embark all the levies of that part, wishing not to start until he had collected the whole force of men and horses destined for his enterprise.

On July 22 Piali and Ali returned to the Salines with the reinforcements, which were landed at once, and on the next day Mustafa marched from the Salines with his whole force towards Nicosia. He had, it was said, 4000 cavalry, 6000 Janissaries, 4000 *Sipahi*, and many adventurers, of whom the number was unknown. The army marched not without fear of some ambush: it seemed to them they had all too easily made themselves masters of the adjoining country. On the 25th the infantry encamped round Nicosia, and on the following day came the cavalry, except 500 who were sent to attack Famagusta. When the force was united before Nicosia they pitched their tents in the open country, and on the hills of Mandia, where was set Mustafa's pavilion, and here they dug very deep wells, from which rose an inexhaustible supply of water. A great part of the force, and particularly the cavalry, were posted towards St Clement, where the water of the citadel takes its rise: there were tents too at the villages of Galanga [Eilenje or Aglanja] and Calassa [Athalassa] five miles away from Nicosia, on account of the water which was found there in plenty.

In Niçosia were:

The Lieutenant of Cyprus, Nicolo Dandolo.

The Count of Carpasso, Collateral of the Signory.

Piero Pisani
Marc' Antonio di Priuli } Councillors.

Zuan Longo
Antonio Pasqualigo } Chamberlains.

Piero Albini, Great Chancellor.

Gio. Battista Colomba.

Cav. Maggi, Engineer.

500 *Stradiot* horse.

Provisionati } 500 horse, and a number of the native
Feudataries } levies (*Cernide*).

Col. Palazzo, commanding 1300 Italian infantry.

Capt. Piovene, of Vicenza.

Alberto Scotto.

Gio. Falier.

Capt. Pocopani, and other Italian gentlemen and soldiers, and many natives.

Mustafa was now encamped before Nicosia, and the first thing the Turks did when they were united in their camp was to begin to ride up to the fortress to invite the defenders to skirmish, but the Collateral would allow no one to go out, but once only when Captain Cortese, a *Stradiot*, was taken prisoner; and the Turks, seeing the citizens did not intend to come out to skirmish, began to build forts. The first was built on the hills of St Maria, 130 paces from the Podocataro bastion, run up with the greatest possible haste, and with little hindrance from within, although from the curtain between the Podocataro and Caraffa bastions, and from the front of the bastion itself, we tried with pieces of 80 to prevent its completion, but it was made by night in spite of our fire. From this fort were attacked the houses, and part of the platforms of the curtains, with small loss of life. The second fort was set at St George of Magnana, and from this too the houses were bombarded: we were forced to give up defending them, though beyond destroying the houses little damage was done. The third was on the hillock called Margheritti, between the Costanzo and Podocataro bastions. The fourth was in the middle of the hill or mount Tomandia. From these forts they could not properly bombard the walls, but they pushed on from them, and came up to the ditch, and to the borders of the old city, and thence with trenches to the bases of the four bastions Podocataro, Costanzo, Davila and Tripoli, about which they planted four other forts, very handy and only 80 paces from the ditch. From these with pieces of 60 they kept up for four days running a brisk fire from morn to night, except for four hours from mid-day, when they rested on account of the excessive heat, and also to let the guns cool.

Mustafa, seeing that the artillery did not answer his expec-

tations, because the shots buried themselves harmlessly in the
soil without injuring the walls, began to approach Nicosia with
spades and shovels, digging very deep trenches.   On our side
from within we attacked them with our cannon, and did great
damage, dislodging and disabling several Turkish guns ; for all
that they came up to the counterscarp, about which they made
a wide trench, throwing up the earth towards the city, and
in it they posted a crowd of musketeers, who fired day and
night on all who showed themselves on the walls.   The Turkish
trenches were guarded all round by ditches and broad and
deep excavations which could hold great bodies of armed men,
which neither guns, horse or foot availed to annoy or throw
into disorder without greater losses on our side.   The enemy
then began to creep up with very deep trenches within the
ditch of the city, throwing up the earth towards the flanks,
where these could batter and damage them.   They made huge
traverses with earth and faggots which their cavalry brought
in from a distance, and with them they blocked our flanks
till they were powerless for harm.   Then they began to tear
down the faces and angles of the bastions.

When the defenders saw that things looked serious, and
that anything might happen, they made a spirited sally with
part of the villagers, townsfolk and Italians.   On August 15
at mid-day (as arranged, because in the morning the Turks
were always at their posts, alert and armed, but from mid-day
on slept or rested in the shade) there went forth 1000 foot-
soldiers, commanded by Captain Piovene, of Vicenza, Lieutenant of the Collateral, who though he served on horseback
willed that day to go out on foot, with Count Alberto Scotto,
and other officers and brave soldiers, both Italians and Greeks,
who marched up to the enemy's posts, and captured two forts,
which the Turks abandoned, thinking perhaps our numbers
greater than they were.   The excitement caused by this success
was such that up to the very tents there was so great confusion
that most of the enemy turned to flight.   But because the

Turkish cavalry came up before our own had left the gates—
they should, according to the orders given, have come out
to support the infantry—we were forced to make an untoward retreat, leaving Captain Piovene and Alberto Scotto
dead, and the Lieutenant of Captain Pocopani, with about 100
others, Italians and Greeks, prisoners. The rest retreated
through the same gate, bringing in Turkish arquebuses, scimi-
tars, and other booty. From that day forth we made no more
sallies, the risk was too great; so needs must, we allowed the
enemy to come up and work what harm they could.

With the consent of the Colonel di Fano, and on his plan,
we made the redoubts on the two bastions Podocataro and
Costanzo, by narrowing the throats of these bastions. In those
of Davila and Tripoli we followed the orders of Gio. Sozomeno,
and made a simple place of retreat without leaving any foot-
hold for the enemy. But we could no longer prevent the
Turks from making an easy and even ramp by which to attack
now one, now two bastions, and even four at once. They
were ever repulsed valiantly, with great losses on either side,
and great waste of rockets and other fireworks, and we were
compelled at last to write in cypher to Famagusta begging
for additional infantry. No answer came, and we feared our
messengers were taken prisoners; and this proved true, for
they were paraded before us by the Turks, that seeing help
to be impossible we might surrender. We were obliged at
last to send Captain Gio. Battista Colomba, a man of weight
and resource, who went and returned at great risk to himself
and no manner of benefit to us. To the same effect we wrote
to the people in the hills, and these messengers too were
captured.

Before dawn on Saturday, September 8, at Mustafa's
request, every galley at the Salines landed 100 of its men,
who marched together to Nicosia under the command of
Ali. He arrived at the 22nd hour of the same day with
a force of about 20,000, and was received by Mustafa with

great joy and all honour. At dawn on Sunday, the 9th, they made a brisk attack on the four bastions. Caraman Pasha, with his Caramanian troop, on Podocataro, Muzaffer Pasha on Constanzo; and on Davila and Tripoli Mustafa and Ali Pashas, with the men from the fleet. All these at one moment with a mighty rush made the attack. The defenders, as they always did, met the charge with great bravery and repulsed the enemy before they could get over the parapet, with fierce slaughter on both sides, but far more among the Turks (although we did not know of the reinforcements they had received from the galleys). At last after a long struggle on the Podocataro bastion by some mishap many of the enemy got in, and captured the platform and the redoubt. In a moment many officers and men were cut to pieces after a stout defence, while some of the villagers, of the *Cernide*, got down through the embrasures and by the curtain, and ran away. As soon as they heard the noise and outcry the Collateral and his brothers, with Colonel Palazzo and other gentlemen, ran to the help of that bastion, but they were too late. Still they drove back the foe with great spirit, but the number of the Turks was too great, and they and all their escort were killed. The other bastions held out till the Turks got into the heart of the city and took them in the rear, pressing in through the throats of the bastions. Then followed that sad and terrible spectacle, the savage slaughter of the poor soldiers who had defended the city, and the nobles, who made a brave stand. They were surrounded and found no way of escape. A few did get away, and in the throats of the bastions and on the narrow platforms, with some of the townsmen, stood their ground valiantly. There was confused fighting in every quarter of the city, and in the squares. There was no order, no one to take the lead, and the massacre lasted till the sixth hour. Those who defended themselves were killed, those who surrendered were made prisoners. At last Mustafa Pasha entered the city, and saw the frightful slaughter. There were many men still with arms in their hands in the Palace square—the bishop of Paphos was slain as he tried to enter it—and in many other places. Mustafa ordered his men to cease from fighting, and exhorted the Christians to yield, promising them their lives. Many surrendered; others, rather than yield them a prey to so savage a tyrant, preferred to die under arms, proving their courage, and avenging themselves in some degree on the foe. At last some 25 or 30 of the nobles remained alive, a few only of the burghers, but all of these were enslaved.

The piteous sack of the ill-fated city was over. Ali took leave of Mustafa, and returned with the men whom he had brought from the fleet: they were embarked on their several galleys, and all the vessels went to the gardens, three miles from Famagusta. Before leaving Nicosia Mustafa installed in the fortress a garrison of 4000 foot soldiers and 1000 cavalry under Muzaffer Pasha, and then started with the main army for Famagusta.

Report of all that befell at FAMAGUSTA wherein are described
most minutely all the Skirmishes, Batteries, Mines and
Assaults given to the said Fortress: also the names of the
Captains, the number of the slain, Christians and Turks
alike: likewise of those who were left in captivity.

Venice, by George Angelieri, M.D.LXXII.

REPORT MADE BY SIGN. COUNT NESTOR MARTI-NENGO OF ALL THAT BEFELL AT FAMAGUSTA TO THE MOST SERENE PRINCE OF VENICE.

[I, Nestore Martinengo, in obedience to the commands
of your Serene Highness, proceed to set down in writing the
whole story of Famagusta from the time of the reinforcements sent there from Venice: for I went thither with Signor
Hieronimo Martinengo at the beginning of this war, and
remained there throughout. I shall pass by all that happened
before this, and exert myself only to give an account of later
events, so far as my memory serves me.]

On February 16, 1571, sailed again the vessels which
brought relief to Famagusta, where there were altogether
4000 footmen, 800 *Cernide*, 3000 citizens and villagers, and
200 Albanians, and on all hands, with greater zeal than before,
the work of fortification went on; the whole garrison, the
burghers, the very chiefs, sparing no toil and labour for the
encouragement of all. By day and by night they visited the
watches to see that the city was duly guarded, and only
exceptionally they went to skirmish outside, just to learn the

enemy's plans. And while such order was taken within, with no less diligence the enemy outside were laying up everything that was needed to storm the fortress, such as great store of woolpacks, wood, artillery, tools and the like, which were brought over with all speed from Caramania and Syria.

At the beginning of April Ali Pasha arrived with about 80 galleys, bringing what was still wanting to the Turks, and sailed again, leaving 30 of the ships which kept crossing to and fro, bringing over men and victuals, with everything else that was required: and besides these a large number of *Caramusolini*, lighters and horseboats kept coming and going from the neighbouring coasts, and this with great speed, fearing always the Christian fleet.

In the middle of the same month 15 pieces of ordnance were brought from Nicosia, the camp was moved from its place, trenches and ditches were dug, and the tents pitched in the gardens, and more towards the west, beyond a place called Precipola. On April 25 they made earthworks to mount the cannon, and trenches for the arquebusiers, one close to the other, drawing nearer very gradually in such a way that we could not hinder them, and working, chiefly at night, with never less than 40,000 pioneers. When we saw the enemy's plan, and where they contemplated their attack, unceasing efforts were made within to meet it. A strong guard was kept posted in the covered way of the counterscarp, and in the salley-ports to defend the counterscarp: new flanks were dug out, and traverses made on the platforms, and all along that part of the wall which received the Turkish fire a trench was made of brick, two feet high and of the same breadth, with loopholes for the arquebusiers who defended the counterscarp. The illustrious Bragadino, with Baglione, gave these matters their personal attention, and admirable order prevailed. All the bread for the soldiers was made in one place, and here presided the illustrious Messer Lorenzo Tiepolo, Captain of Paphos, who spared himself no kind of trouble. In the Castle

was the right-worshipful Messer Andrea Bragadino, who with
all diligence watched the guarding of the sea-front, repairing
the flanks and digging out new ones to protect the quarter
of the arsenal. The Commander of the artillery was Cav.
Goito, who lost his life just now in a skirmish; the right-
worshipful Bragadino gave me his company. Three captains
were set over the fireworks, with 20 footmen apiece, chosen
from the companies to handle the explosives. All the serviceable cannon were moved to the quarter where the attack
was expected, and platforms were provided for the embrasures.
We failed not to make frequent sallies in all directions to annoy
the enemy, and we did them no little injury. On one occasion,
when charging out with 300 citizens armed with sword and
shield, and a like number of Italian arquebusiers, we suffered
great losses because the enemy's trenches were too thickly set,
and although we routed them and slew many, they sprung up
in such hosts that they killed 30 of our men, and wounded
60. After this we made no more sallies, the risk was too
great. Gradually the enemy brought their trenches to the top
of the counterscarp, and having completed their batteries, on
May 19 they began the attack from 10 forts on which were
mounted 74 pieces of great ordnance, among them four
so-called basilisks of enormous size. The plan of attack
ranged from the Limasol gate to the Arsenal, which was covered
by five guns on the fort of the rock, another on the curtain of
the Arsenal over against a fort of 11 guns, another on the
great tower of the Andruzzi with the two cavaliers above it from
a fort mounting also 11 guns, another on the great tower of
St Nappa, which had to face the fire of the four basilisks. The
Limasol gate, which had a tall cavalier atop and a ravelin
beyond, was bombarded by the forts with 33 cannon, under
the orders of Mustafa the general commanding-in-chief.

At the outset they hardly troubled about destroying the
walls, but they fired on the city, and at our guns, which were
doing them great damage. This caused all the soldiers and

Greeks to take up their quarters on the walls, and there they remained to the end. The most worshipful Bragadino lodged in the great tower of the Andrucci, Signor Baglione in that of St Nappa, the most worshipful Tiepolo in that of Campo Santo. So they were present at all the engagements, and dealt out encouragement or rebuke where each was necessary. Signor Luigi Martinengo was put in command of the artillery, a man of great worth, who told off the gates to six captains, who looked after their men and all that was needful for the bombardiers, a company of Greeks being posted at each gate to serve the guns. Captain Francesco Bogone was on duty at the great tower and the great cavalier of the Arsenal. Captain Piatro Conte was on duty on the curtain, at the cavalier de' Volti, and the great tower of Campo Santo. I was in charge of the cavalier of Campo Santo, of that of the Andruzzi, and of the curtain as far as the great tower of St Nappa. Count Hercole Martinengo of the cavalier of St Nappa, and all the curtain up to the Limasol gate. At the ravelin and curtain towards the bulwark was Captain Oratio da Veletri, while Captain Roberto Malvezzi was in charge of the tall cavalier of Limasol, which received the fiercest cannonade. At the time the attack began, by order of the most worshipful Bragadino, victuals were served out to all the soldiers, Greeks and Italians alike, and to the gunners, wine, soup, cheese and salted meat; everything was brought to the walls in excellent order, so that a soldier spent no more than two soldi a day in bread. Pay was issued every thirty days, the illustrious M. Gio. Antonio Querini giving it his particular attention: and besides this duty he was present at every action of importance, to encourage the troops. For ten days we replied to their fire with such fury that 15 of their best pieces were disabled, and some 30,000 Turks slain. They were no longer safe in their entrenchments, and panic reigned among them; but we saw that our powder was getting low, a limit was fixed, and no more than 30 shots were fired daily from each of 30 guns, and always in the presence of the captains, that no shot might be wasted.

On May 29 a frigate came from Candia, bringing hopes of succour, and giving great encouragement to all. The enemy had won the counterscarp after a sharp fight and losses on both sides: thereon to meet our five batteries they began to take the earth round the walls of the counterscarp, and to throw it into the ditch; while we carried off by night within the walls all that soil and the wreckage of the walls caused by their fire; we were all at work on this until the enemy opened some loopholes in the wall, through which their arquebusiers swept all the ditch, and prevented our approaching it any more without great risk. But M. Gio. Mormori, an engineer, invented a plan of joining planks which were carried so as to protect the workers from musket fire. Earth was still brought in, but a little only, and Messer Giovanni himself was killed: he had rendered excellent service in all our needs. The Turks had now thrown up enough earth to reach the top of the ditch: they made an opening in the wall of the counterscarp, and piling up the earth before them they gradually made a traverse up to the wall on both sides of all our batteries, and strengthened it later with woolpacks and fascines, to protect themselves against our flanking fire. They now held the ditch so that they could not be molested except from above, and that only by chance, and they began to dig mines at the ravelin, at the great tower of St Nappa, at those of the Andruzzi and Campo Santo, at the curtain, and the great tower of the Arsenal. As we could make no more use of our few flanks we cast fireworks among the enemy which worked great havoc; the woolpacks and fascines were set on fire, and to those who managed to destroy the packs Bragadino gave a ducat for each. Counter-mines were laid in all directions under the orders of Cav. Maggio, an engineer, who worked throughout with all possible diligence and energy. But they crossed only with those of the great towers of St Nappa, of the Andruzzi and Campo Santo, for these were empty, and many sallies were made by day and night into the ditch, to spy out the mines and set fire to the fascines and woolpacks. The wonderful energy and toil of Signor Baglione, who looked after all these matters, was never wanting in infinite devices for harassing the foe. He divided the companies between the batteries, adding at each point a company of Albanians, who proved their worth both as horse and foot soldiers.

FIRST ATTACK.

On June 21 they fired the mine under the great tower of the Arsenal, which was in charge of Janpulad bey: it shattered the wall, which was of great thickness, breached it, and brought down more than half of it, splitting also a part of the parapet which had been made to project and face an attack, and straightway a great number of Turks climbed on the ruins and reached the top with their ensigns. Captain Pietro Conte was on guard with his company which was much shaken by the explosion. I and my company were first on the spot, and they were repulsed: and though the enemy brought up fresh troops four or five times they did not attain their aim. Signor Baglione was engaged in person, and the most worshipful Bragadino and the illustrious Querini stood under arms some little distance away to encourage the men: and the illustrious Castellano with the guns of the spur inflicted great losses on the enemy throughout the attack, which lasted for five hours without a break. A great number of the Turks were killed, and we lost in dead and wounded about 100, through an accident to our fireworks which through careless handling burned many of our men. Among the dead were Count Gio. Francesco Goro, Captain Bernardino Ugubio: Signor Hercole Malatesta, Captain Pietro Conte, and other captains and ensigns, were badly wounded by stones. The following night a frigate arrived from Candia, bringing news of sure and certain aid, and spreading general joy and encourage-

ment.   Under the guidance of Captain Marco Crivelatore and
of Cav. Maggio flanked redoubts were added to all the points
attacked, and where mining could be heard we set barrels full
of wet earth, boxes, mattresses and sacks full of wet earth—
(for the Greeks with great promptness had brought all they
had, for when the canvas was used up they brought hangings,
curtains, carpets, and even their sheets to make these sacks)
an excellent and speedy way of rebuilding the parapets which
were wrecked by the fury of their artillery fire, which was never
silent.   All that was destroyed at night was rebuilt by day, for
the soldiers got no sleep, and were always alert on the wall,
visited continually by their chiefs, who slept only during the
hottest hours of the day, for they had no other time for rest, as
the enemy were calling at every moment to arms, to leave us
no respite.

Second Attack.

On June 29 the mine made in the stonework of the ravelin
was fired, shattering everything and doing immense damage,
besides giving an easy ascent to the enemy, who rushed wildly
to the crest, Mustafa being present throughout.   Count Hercole
Martinengo and his company met the first shock, and so the
Turks were repulsed by our men, who fought in the open, for
the parapet was destroyed by the mine.   On our side there
fell Captain Meani, Sergeant Major, Captain Celio of the
Grenadiers, Captain Erasmo da Fermo, Captain Soldatello,
Antonio d' Ascoli, Captain Gio. d' Istria : many ensigns and
officers were wounded, and about 30 soldiers killed.   At the
Arsenal the Turks were repulsed with greater loss on their side
and less on ours.   Five only were killed, among them Captain
Giacomo da Fabiano, and I was struck by a musket ball in
the left leg.   The attack lasted six hours, and the bishop
of Limasol stood there with the cross cheering on the soldiers,
and there were brave women with arms, stones and water to
help the combatants.   The enemy, seeing the great losses

they had suffered in these two attacks, changed their plan, and with greater fury than ever began again to batter our defences and shelters at all points, working more actively than ever. They made seven new forts closer under the fortress, brought up the guns from the more distant works, and mounted 80 fresh pieces. On the day and night of July 8 their fire was so brisk that 5000 shots were counted, and they shattered our parapets till it was only with immense toil that we could repair them, for our labourers were killed one after another by cannon-shot, or by the incessant hail of musketry, and but few were left. The shelter behind the ravelin was so damaged by shots and mines that no platform was left, because in strengthening the parapets from within we encroached on the platform, which we were obliged to lengthen with planks. Captain Maggio constructed a mine under this ravelin, so that when we could no longer hold it, we might abandon it to the enemy, and inflict on him some signal damage.

Third Attack.

On July 9 they made the third assault on the ravelin, on the great tower of St Nappa and that of the Andruzzi, on the curtain and great tower of the Arsenal. It lasted over six hours, and at all four points the Turks were driven back, but the ravelin was abandoned with great loss on both sides. The defenders could not in that small space use their pikes to any purpose, and when they wanted to retire, according to the order given by Signor Baglione, they fell into disorder, and retreated mixed up with the Turks. Our mine was fired, and we saw with horror the destruction of more than 1000 of the enemy, and more than 100 of our men. Captain Roberto Malvezzi died on the spot, and Captain Marchetto of Fermo was grievously wounded: at the attack on the Arsenal Captain David Noce the Quartermaster was killed, and I was wounded by a splinter. This attack lasted five long hours, and at all points the people of Famagusta showed great valour, as well as their women and children. The ravelin was so shattered by the explosion that no further effort was made to retake it, for there was nothing left as a shelter. The left flank only was left standing, and here we dug another mine. Opposite the ravelin was the Limasol gate, a lower work, which was always kept open, for it had an iron portcullis, very heavy and studded with sharp points, closed by cutting a rope. We tried to carry in the earth of the ravelin by this gate, and for four days the Turks did not approach it; afterwards they began to entrench themselves anew on higher ground, and from the upper flanks they prevented anyone from leaving the gate, which they watched very carefully, because they were frequently attacked by our troops.

Fourth Attack.

So on July 14 they came up to attack the gate, and after a charge at all the other batteries they marched up to plant their ensigns right in front of the gate. Signor Baglione and Signor Luigi, who had undertaken the defence of that post, were present and cheered on the soldiers who burst forth and killed and put to flight the greater part of the enemy. They fired the mine in the flank, which slew about 400 Turks, and Signor Baglione captured one of the enemy's standards, wresting it from the hands of its bearer. The next day they fired the mine under the curtain but the result was of little profit to them, and they refrained from delivering a set attack, and went on widening and raising the traverses in the ditches to protect them in future attacks. They had dug out all the earth near the counterscarp, and there they encamped with their tents, which we could not see. They brought up seven pieces of artillery on the wall of the counterscarp so disposed that we could not see them; two on the ravelin of the great tower of St Nappa, one on the Andruzzi, and two facing the battery of the curtain. They came with planks covered with raw hide to dig in the parapets, while we were not slow in hurling grenades among them, and in sallying now and then from the shelters to harass the diggers, but our losses were considerable. We restored the parapets with buffalo skins soaked in water and stuffed with earth, waste and wet cotton, well bound with cords.

All the women of Famagusta, under the guidance of a monk, made up companies for each quarter of the city, and went every day to work at the post assigned to them, carrying stones and water, which was stored in half casks in every battery to quench the fire thrown by the Turks. For having failed to take the gate, they found a wholly new device. They collected a great quantity of wood called *teglia* which burns easily with a bad smell: this they piled before the gate, lighted it, and with fascines and beams smeared with pitch they worked up so fierce a fire that it was impossible to extinguish it, though we kept throwing casks full of water from the tall cavalier which burst over the fire. This lasted four days when by reason of the great heat and stench our men were forced to retire into the city. The Turks went down into the lower flanks, and began to dig fresh mines. We closed the gate, which we could no longer leave open, and straightway to the surprise of all they remade the platform of the ravelin and planted a gun over against the gate, which our men had entirely earthed up with stones, earth and other material.

The position of the city was now desperate; within the walls everything was lacking except hope, the valour of the commanders, the daring of the soldiers. The wine was exhausted, neither fresh nor salted meat nor cheese could be had, except at extravagant prices. The horses, asses and cats were consumed. There was nothing to eat but bread and beans, nothing to drink but vinegar and water, and this too soon failed. The digging of fresh mines was heard below in the cavalier of the gate: everywhere the enemy was toiling with more activity than ever: in the ditch opposite the battery of the curtain they kept heaping up a mound of earth as high as the wall, and before long they reached the wall of the counterscarp: opposite the great tower of the Arsenal they constructed a cavalier, all strengthened without with cables, as high as that of the city.

Within the walls were left about 500 Italian soldiers, sound, but worn with long watches and the toil of fighting under the blazing sun: the most and best of the Greeks were dead, and about July 20 the chief men of Famagusta resolved to write to the right worshipful Bragadino, entreating him that now the fortress was reduced to such a pass, its defenders gone, its supplies spent, with no hope of assistance, since they had sacrificed their lives and goods in pursuit of their safety and their allegiance to the republic, he would agree to terms of honourable surrender, with due regard to the honour of their wives, and the lives of their children, who would be left in the enemy's clutches. Bragadino answered with words of consolation and encouragement, promising that help would come, allaying as far as he could the general terror that prevailed, and sending at their request a frigate to Candia to announce the straits they were in.

The Turks had finished their mines, and fired them on July 29. In the meanwhile the defenders had been trying as usual to restore the parapets which the cannonade had shattered, and as there was no other material left the sacks were made of *carisea* under the superintendence of the illustrious Tiepolo. The three mines of the cavalier did great damage, throwing down the greater portion of the work, and killing the Governor Rondacchi. The mine at the Arsenal shattered the rest of the great tower, blowing up nearly a whole company of our soldiers: only the two flanks remained whole.

Fifth Attack.

The enemy strove to take these two flanks, and to mount on the other batteries: the attack lasted from the twentieth hour until night, and very many Turks were killed. In this fight and others Signor Giacomo Strambali showed great valour, and so did others.

Sixth Attack.

The next morning at dawn the city was attacked at all points. This assault lasted six hours, with very little loss on our side for the Turks fought with less spirit than usual. They kept giving us great trouble on the seafront with their galleys, firing at every attack, and battering every part of the city which they could reach. This assault was warded off, but the city was reduced to great straits, only seven barrels of powder were left, so the chiefs resolved to surrender under honourable conditions.

On August 1, when noon was passed, a truce was made, and an envoy came from Mustafa Pasha, with whom it was agreed that the following morning two hostages should be given on either side while the agreement was under discussion. By order of the right worshipful Bragadino there went out as hostages on our side Count Hercole Martinengo, and Signor Matteo Colfi, a citizen of Famagusta, and from the enemy's camp there came into the city the lieutenants of Mustafa and of the *Agha* of the Janissaries, who were met at the gate by Signor Baglione with 200 musketeers, while our officers were met by the Turks with a great array of cavalry and musketeers, accompanied by Mustafa's son in person, who welcomed them with courtesy. Signor Baglione discussed the terms of capitulation with the Turkish hostages in the city. He asked for the lives of the defenders, their arms, their goods: five cannon, three of their finest horses, and a safe passage to Candia under an escort of galleys: that the Greeks should stay in their houses and enjoy what was their own, living like Christians. The Turks accepted these conditions, to which Mustafa assented and signed the truce. They forthwith sent galleys and sailing ships into the harbour, the soldiers began to embark, and when most of them were on board, the captains being anxious also to embark, on the morning of August 15 the right worshipful Bragadino sent me with a letter to Mustafa to say that the same evening he proposed to come out to hand to him the keys of the city, leaving the right worshipful Tiepolo in charge of the fortress. He begged that during his absence nothing should be done to annoy the citizens, for up to this time Turks and Christians had maintained with each other friendly and trustful intercourse, in all courtesy of deed and word. Mustafa replied verbally desiring me to tell the right worshipful Bragadino to come when he pleased: that he would gladly see and know him, for he recognised the great courage shown by him, his fellow officers and brave soldiers, whom, wherever he was, he should never fail to praise. On no account, let them be assured, would he suffer any annoyance to be inflicted on the citizens. I returned and reported accordingly.

In the evening, about the 21st hour, the right worshipful Bragadino, accompanied by Signor Baglione, Signor Alouigi, the illustrious Signor Gio. Anton Querini, the illustrious Signor Andrea Bragadino, Cav. dalle Haste, Cap. Carlo Ragonasco, Cap. Franc. Straco, Cap. Hettor da Brescia, Cap. Girolamo di Sacile, and other gentlemen, with 50 soldiers, went out: the officers wore their swords, the soldiers had muskets. So they went to Mustafa's tent, who at first received them courteously and made them sit down. They passed from one subject to another, then a complaint arose that during the truce Signor Bragadino had caused certain slaves to be put to death. There was not a word of truth in it, but Mustafa rising in anger would scarcely listen to what his visitors said, and ordered them to be bound. They were defenceless, for

they were compelled to lay aside their arms before entering
the tent, and thus bound were led one by one into the open
square before the tent, and cut to pieces in Mustafa's presence.
Then twice and thrice he made Signor Bragadino, who showed
no sign of fear, stretch out his neck as though he would strike
off his head, but spared his life and cut off his ears and nose,
and as he lay on the ground Mustafa reviled him, cursing our
Saviour and saying "where now is thy Christ that He doth
not help thee?" The general made never an answer. Count
Hercole, one of the hostages, was also bound, but was hidden
by one of Mustafa's eunuchs until his chief's fury was passed.
He spared his life and made him his slave. There were three
Greeks in the tent who were released, but the soldiers present
in the Turkish camp were hewed in pieces, with 300 other
Christians, who never dreamed of such gross perfidy and
savagery. The Christians who were already embarked were
thrown into chains and robbed.

The second day after the murders, August 17, Mustafa
first entered the city. He caused the most worshipful Tiepolo
to be hanged. I, who was in the city when the rest were
slaughtered and enslaved, lay hid in Greek houses five days;
but when I got no more shelter, the penalties were too great,
I surrendered as a slave to a Sanjaq of Bir, with whom I stayed
in the camp, my ransom being fixed at 500 sequins. On
August 17, being a Friday and their holiday, Signor Bragadino
was led, Mustafa being present throughout, to the batteries
built against the city and was made to carry one basket full of
earth up, and another down, on each fort, and made to kiss
the ground when he passed before Mustafa. Then he was led
to the shore, set in a slung seat, and hoisted on the yard of
a galley hung "like a stork" in view of all the slaves and
Christian soldiers in the port. He was then led to the square,
stripped, made to sit on the grating of the pillory, and brutally
flayed alive. He bore all with great firmness and faith, never
losing heart but ever with the sternest constancy reproaching

them for their broken faith. With never a sign of wavering he commended himself to God, and gave back his spirit to his Maker. His skin was taken and stuffed with straw, and hung on the yard of a galliot, was paraded along the coast of Syria. This is all I can tell your Serene Highness from memory of what happened while I was in the fortress. What I heard from good sources, and what I saw while I was a slave in the camp, I will set down briefly.

The Turkish host numbered 200,000 persons of every rank and condition, of whom 80,000 were paid soldiers, besides the 14,000 Janissaries drawn from all the garrisons of Syria, Caramania, Anatolia and even from the Porte. The armed adventurers were 60,000, their vast numbers being due to the reports which Mustafa had spread through the Turkish territory that Famagusta was far richer than Nicosia; and as the passage was so easy they were tempted across. In the 75 days of the siege 150,000 iron balls were seen and counted. The chief personages who accompanied Mustafa were the Pasha of Aleppo, the Pasha of Anatolia, Muzaffer Pasha, of Nicosia, the Pasha of Caramania, the *Agha* of the Janissaries, Janpulad bey, the Sanjaq of Tripoli, the Beylerbey of Greece, the Pasha of Sivas and Marash, Ferca Framburaro, the Sanjaq of Antippo, Suleiman bey, three Sanjaqs of Arabia, Mustafa bey, General of the Adventurers, the Fergat, Lord of Malatia, the Framburaro of Divrigi. Of these were killed the Pasha of Anatolia, Mustafa, General of the Adventurers, the Sanjaq of Tripoli, Fergat, Lord of Malatia, the Framburaro of Antipo, the Framburaro of Divrigi, the Sanjaq of Arabia, and other lesser Sanjaqs, with a host of 80,000 men, according to an account taken by Mustafa's orders. They left the Framburaro who was at Rhodes as Governor of Famagusta, and it was said they proposed to leave in all the island 20,000 men, with 2000 horses, poor beasts and out of condition. I saw them myself.

It beseems me yet not to omit how by the grace of God

I was delivered out of their hands, having within the period of the 42 days of my slavery paid the ransom of 500 sequins with the aid of the consul of the French merchants who came from Tripoli to the camp. My master was unwilling to give me up, saying that he wanted to take me to his Sanjaq on the Euphrates, and then let me go. I, knowing his bad heart, decided to escape, and being allowed sometimes to go into the city I hired a boat from a Greek sailor, and in one night, with two oars and something of a sail made out of two shirts, we got over to Tripoli in Syria, at no small risk of drowning; and there I lay hid in the house of some Christians, until on September 25 I left the place in a small French vessel, called *St Victor*, which traded on those coasts. We touched in the west of Cyprus at Cape delle Gatte, where I landed and talked to some peasants who were hawking. I asked them how they were treated by the Turks, and how the island was tilled and sown. They replied that they could not be worse treated, for they were always brutally handled and beaten; they recognised now the gentle rule of the Christians, and prayed they might return. That all that was cultivated of the island was the mountainous region towards the west, because they were little molested there by the Turks, but in the open country and towards the east there was little tillage, and the land was like a desert, for there were few inhabitants and small store of cattle. Thence we reached Candia. I was clothed in sackcloth, but there by the kindness of the illustrious Signor Latino Orsino I was dressed and graciously tended. From Candia in a Cypriot vessel I arrived, by God's mercy, in safety in this city, and at your Highness' feet. [Assuring your Highness that not the toils and watches of so long a siege, not the wounds received on those walls, not the heavy cost incurred in all that time, in my ransom, and in the loss of all my goods, nor yet my cruel servitude with the Turks, have chilled one whit my spirit: nay, it is more than ever inflamed to expose this life of mine again a thousand times to every kind of danger, as I have done on this first occasion. So I commend myself humbly to your kind favour.]

CHRISTIAN CAPTAINS KILLED AT FAMAGUSTA.

Signor Estore Baglione.
  „ Aluigi Martinengo.
  „ Federico Baglione.
Caval. dall' Asta, Vice-Governor.
Ca. Davit Noce, Quartermaster.
Cap. Mignano, of Perugia, Sergeant-Major.
Count Sigismondo da Casoldo.
Count Francesco di Lobi, of Cremona.
Cap. Francesco Troncauilla.
Ca. Annibale Adamo, of Fermo.
Ca. Scipione, of Città di Castello.
Ca. Carlo Ragonasco, of Cremona.
Cap. Francesco Straco.
Cap. Ruberto Malvezzo.
Ca. Cesare de Aduerca.
Cap. Bernardino, of Agubio.
Ca. Francesco Bugon, of Verona.
Ca. Jacobo de Fabiano.
Cap. Bastian dal Sole, a Florentine.
Ca. Ettor da Brescia, who succeeded Cap. C. d' Aduerca.
Cap. Flaminio, of Florence, who succeeded Cap. B. dal Sole.
Cap. Erasmo, of Fermo, who succeeded Cap. dalle Cernole.
Cap. Bartolomeo dalle Cernole.
Cap. Gio. Battista, of Rivarole.
Cap. Giouan Francesco, of Venice.

NAMES OF CAPTAINS ENSLAVED.

Count Ercole Martinengo, with Giulio Cesar Ghelfo, a Brescian soldier.

Count Nestor Martinengo, escaped.

Cap. Marco Crivellatore.

Sig. Ercole Malatista.

Cap. Pier, Count of Montalberto.

Cap. Oratio, of Veletri.

Cap. Aluigi Pezano.

Count Jacobo della Corbara.

Cap. Giouan d' Istria.

Cap. Soldatello, of Agubio.

Cap. Giouan, of Ascoli.

Cap. Antonio, of Ascoli.

Cap. Bastian, of Ascoli.

Cap. Salgano, of Città di Castello.

Cap. Marquess of Fermo.

Cap. Gio. Antonio, of Piacenza.

Cap. Carletto Naldo.

Cap. Lorenzo Fornaretti.

Cap. Bernardo, of Brescia.

Cap. Bernardino Coco.

Cap. Simone Bagnese, who succeeded Cap. David Noce.

Cap. Tiberio Ceruto, who succeeded Count Sigismondo.

Ca. Gioseppe, of Lanciano, who succeeded Cap. Fr. Troncavilla.

Cap. Morgante, who succeeded Ca. Annibale.

The Lieutenant who succeeded Cap. Scipione.

The Ensign who succeeded Cap. R. Malvetio.

Cap. Ottavio, of Rimini, who succeeded Cap. Fr. Bugon.

Cap. Mario, of Fabiano, who succeeded Cap. Jacomo.

Cap. Francesco, of Venice, who succeeded Cap. Antonio.

Cap. Matteo, of Capua.

Cap. Gio. Maria, of Verona.
Cap. Mancino.

ENGINEERS.

Giouanni Mormori, killed.
Cav. Girolamo Maggio, of Anghiari, enslaved [escaped, retaken and strangled, March 27, 1572.]

TURKISH CAPTAINS IN FAMAGUSTA.

Mustafa, General.
Pasha of Aleppo.
Pasha of Anatolia, killed.
Muzaffer, Pasha of Nicosia.
Pasha of Caramania.
Agha of the Janissaries.
Janpulad bey.
Sanjaq of Tripoli.
Beylerbey of Greece.
Pasha of Sivas and Marash.
Ferca Framburaro.

Sanjaq of Antipo, killed.
Suleiman bey, killed.
Three Sanjaqs of Arabia, one killed.
Mustafa bey, General of Adventurers, killed.
The Fergat, lord of Malatia, killed.
The Framburaro of Divrigi, killed.

FINIS.

Those who are curious to see how the same episode is set forth for Turks by a Turk can read this short extract which I have translated from *Qibris Tarikhi* (Levqosha, 1312) *Nicosia*, 1895, pp. 89—91.

A. H. 978. Here again the Ottoman troops were set in array, a mine was fired, and fresh cannon kept up the attack, until on the second day of the siege a part of the Fort was brought to the ground, and after a bloody fight maintained for five hours the Venetian General Bragadino was forced to surrender.

In accordance with the truce signed by both sides the effects and arms of the Venetians, together with five cannon, and three horses belonging to the commanding officers, were to be transported on 20 Turkish vessels. The whole population of the island as then enrolled was put at 120,000 males, from each of whom a gold piece was collected as tax.

The General Mustafa Pasha kept suspecting that the warships which were to transport the Venetians might not be sent back, and that possibly during the voyage their crews might be killed.

On our side the vessels were made ready for sea, the Venetians were transporting their effects, and nothing remained but to bid an official farewell to our General. Bragadino asked to have an audience of his Excellency, and leave was granted. On a Friday, about 10 o'clock, the Venetian General, holding a red umbrella on which was an ornament peculiar to the nobles of Venice, and the chiefs of his staff, Baglione, Louis Martino, Anton Querini, with 40 armed knights, came to the General's pavilion: they were received by a guard of honour, and with all state and respect.

Mustafa Pasha asked why he showed no mercy to the Defterdar of Egypt and his staff, who were unjustly slain, and why he gave orders for the execution of all the Moslem prisoners of war who were in the Fort of Famagusta, and on receiving the answer "they were my prisoners, I killed them all"—and when before moving he refused to leave Anton Querini as a hostage, Bragadino and his comrades were by the General's command chained and thrown into prison, and 10 days later, in revenge for the blood of the Defterdar and about 50 pilgrims, they were all executed, and their heads were sent to Constantinople. Afterwards Bragadino's remains were transported to Venice by his relations, and buried in the church of St Gregory.

Europeans, with great exaggeration, tell a long story how, before the body of the victim was flayed—however it was that he killed the Moslem prisoners—his nose and ears were cut off, and then he was slain with tortures. If the case is compared with the frightful cruelties committed by the tribunal of the Inquisition upon the Arabs, it is clear anyhow that the Turks were more merciful than they.

After the conquest of Famagusta Janissaries and Cavalry were posted where and as necessary, and trustworthy commanders left for the protection of the island. The General Lala Mustafa Pasha, taking with him his staff, returned with the fleet to Constantinople. A brilliant deputation was sent to meet him : Selim II offered congratulations and yet higher honours, and the revenues of conquered Cyprus were assigned to the brave Commander.

INDEX

CAMBRIDGE: PRINTED BY JOHN CLAY, M.A. AT THE UNIVERSITY PRESS.